I0082392

MORE FROM THE LONGMYND ADVENTURE CAMP, AND ME

Alan Scriven MBE

HEDDON PUBLISHING

First edition published in 2018 by Heddon Publishing.

Copyright © Alan Scriven 2018, all rights reserved.
No part of this book may be reproduced, adapted, stored in a retrieval
system or transmitted by any means, electronic, photocopying, or otherwise
without prior permission of the author.

ISBN 978-1-9995963-2-3

Cover design by Catherine Clarke

Although the author and publisher have made every effort to ensure that the
information in this book was correct at press time, the author and publisher
do not assume and hereby disclaim any liability to any party for any loss,
damage, or disruption caused by errors or omissions, whether such errors or
omissions result from negligence, accident, or any other cause.

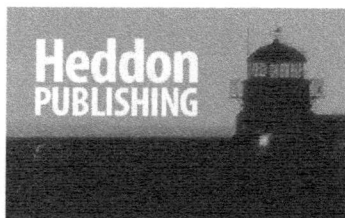

www.heddonpublishing.com
www.facebook.com/heddonpublishing
@PublishHeddon

I am honoured to dedicate this book to the memory of the late Mrs Hetty Williams and also Hetty's and Bill's daughters, Ann Lewis and Debbie Bridge.

Prologue

Following the publication of my first book, *The Longmynd Adventure Camp and Me*, and the interest it received, I was encouraged by more than a few kind souls to continue writing about 'the Camp' and my life. The feeling was that I couldn't possibly have crammed into one book thirty-three years of experience with this once much-loved and needed children's charity, not to mention what was happening in my life, as I walked this challenging but wonderful path.

I also felt it might be worthwhile to bring the reader up-to-date with my understanding of what has happened to the Camp since 1998, and to one or two people who played a major part in its early growth and success but who are sadly not acknowledged in the current committee's *Dawn Chorus* pamphlet(s).

By the end of the book, we will be well into the 21st century.

I considered seriously whether there could be another book within the memory bank of my life, Camp experiences, and other material not featured in my first book. However, I arrived at the conclusion that there possibly was, especially if I included a good collection of correspondence from the Camp beneficiaries, its sponsors, and others; and perhaps also a few newspaper reports from over the years, along with a number of Camp Magazine articles by the staff and boys from the sixties. I also thought it would be good to let some members of staff give the reader a little insight into how they themselves came to be numbered amongst the many kind people who volunteered their help over the Camp's first forty years.

All of the above I considered would provide valuable assistance to me in producing a second, and final, volume about the Longmynd Adventure Camp, and me.

My first book tells a true and concise history of the charity's evolution over its first forty years and features episodes of my personal life as well as my involvement with this amazing place from 1965 until 1998 (when everything changed... not for the better, from my perspective).

The Longmynd Adventure Camp is still very much in existence today (though it bears little or no resemblance to how it looked and operated during my many years as both beneficiary and, later, voluntary member of staff). It is by any standard, however, now a first-class facility for anyone who has the pleasure of using it. And this is down to the present-day committee (and supporters of the charity), which as far as I am aware still numbers Mr Don Rogers (though no longer Chair) and Mr Malcolm Hoad among its members. However, the vast majority of the people who helped to set the Camp up, and saw it through its long teething years, are not even a memory to most of the people involved today.

My first book, being a concise and detailed history of the Camp, included all the 'politics'. My aim with this second book is to tell a more light-hearted story on a familiar topic, combined with a little more of my personal story, which I hope the reader will enjoy just as much. I have also included a brief history of the Women's Royal Voluntary Service (WRVS), focusing on Shropshire and the West Midlands. This much-needed organisation has been very kind to thousands of people since its inception in the 1930s. Without the WRVS, places such as the Longmynd Adventure Camp might never have existed, even with the undoubted commitment of good folk like Bill Williams BEM, and those born under the same charitable star.

I have chosen to begin this book with a few words written by Mr William Frederick Williams BEM (Founder, Committee Chair, and Skipper of the Camp 1958-1989) a few years before he passed away in 2013. Bill began writing his memoirs, despite his constant assumption that no-one would be interested in reading his work. I beg to differ.

Bill's life story (excerpts of which his daughters Ann and Debbie have kindly given me permission me to include), particularly his childhood and early adult years, makes fascinating reading, and I simply couldn't let his words fade into 'quiet oblivion'; he so deserves to be read. Another reason for my inclusion of Bill's words of wisdom is to show the reader exactly why and how Bill created the Camp; and how much his story of early life mirrors my own experiences of extreme poverty, as told in my first book.

This wonderful piece of social history also records how, by complete chance, Bill Williams came to join the police force.

I dedicated *The Longmynd Adventure Camp and Me* to Bill Williams BEM; my mentor, and great friend. I have dedicated this second book to his wife, Hetty. Mrs Williams was a lovely and truly genuine lady whom anyone would be proud to have known. I am exceptionally proud to include myself as a friend of the Williams family, all of whom (but especially Mrs W) gave up many hours of precious time, including family holidays, with Bill. This allowed him to concentrate on making the Camp a huge success story, which brightened the lives of hundreds of boys just like me, from the poorer urban areas of many towns and cities of England.

Hetty, Ann and Debbie all gave their valued help to Bill as and when they were able to; in whatever way they could. But most of all, they gave him the time and space he needed for his dream to succeed.

The Late Great Bill Williams BEM

(In his own words)

When one thinks back to what the living conditions were for the family generations before your own, it is very hard to imagine what their lives must have been like. So far as my family, and most other people that we knew, were concerned, life was hard. No radio, and obviously no television; very little money, and for me, the only 'entertainment' I had was my weekly visit to the Saturday afternoon picture show. And this luxury was only possible because, whilst still at school, I worked on a market stall at weekends.

We played the usual childhood games such as Cowboys and Indians, etc.; for our 'transport' we built trolleys from four old pram wheels and a plank of wood. We also put the trolley to use when two pennyworth of gas coke was needed from the nearby gasworks, to keep the open fire in the house alight.

I was born on 15th September 1926 in Arleston village, near Wellington, Shropshire; but lived for the majority of my childhood at 104 High Street, Wellington. The house was a 'two-up, two-down' terrace type, which was demolished years ago. I remember the rent, at some point, was four shillings a week, and our mum's weekly income, after Dad died, was just ten shillings' 'Widow's Pension'.

There was no National Health Service.

Our front door opened onto the High Street, and the rear door to a yard which I remember as being very large. It is more likely, however, that it appeared so big because I was so young and small!

Living together in this small two-bedroom house were my mother Florence; my father, William Isaac Williams; my elder sister Mary Evelyn; me, and my younger brother David Charles.

My father died aged just 35yrs. My paternal grandparents lived in Blackpool, but my maternal grandmother, Clara Grey, lived near us in Wellington. Details of my maternal grandfather (dead by this time) are very cloudy but it is believed, though not confirmed, that he was of African origin.

There was no water supply to our house, but there was a communal tap outside in the yard. This meant no tap over the kitchen sink, or waste pipe below. The water simply drained into a bucket which was emptied into the drain outside. Our lighting was supplied by gas lamp, complete with mantle.

We had a coal fire in the living room; the old-fashioned type of range with an oven on one side and a small water tank with a tap on the other, which, obviously, had to be filled by hand. The shelf of the oven was metal, and on cold nights this was wrapped in a piece of blanket and used to warm the bed. Mum also placed house bricks in the oven and when heated these were also wrapped and used as bed warmers. There was no bathroom in the house. We had a tin bath, and water had to be heated in the outside communal wash-house, or brew-house as it was called. But more often than not, water was heated in a kettle on the open fire indoors.

The wash-house was used jointly by our family and our neighbours in the terrace. It had a brick-built solid fuel copper boiler which had to be lit, to burn wood and coal on wash days. This room also housed a large old-fashioned mangle, which I sometimes helped to turn, or tried to! I also remember our dolly tub and dolly peg; a far cry from today's machines.

At the top of the yard were the lavatories, which actually were earth closets. No toilet rolls, just a few pieces of newspaper cut up into squares. It was quite a normal procedure during the winter months, and hours of darkness, to carry a candle in a jar to light your way up the yard. Also in the yard was a small piece of garden (no more than about three yards square). It was my first garden. I used it to grow a few flower seeds, such as Californian Poppies, because my mother liked them. It was also used on occasions in our childish play, for burial plots after funeral services for the odd dead bird that we sometimes found.

To supplement our meagre bedclothes in the winter we had at least two very heavy overcoats which were affectionately known as 'Big Ben' and 'Little Len'. There was often a fight of sorts over who had which.

It wasn't uncommon to take a candle to bed to read by. One night I fell asleep, and the candle fell over onto my bed, causing *it to catch fire! But thankfully, Mother came to the rescue, dousing the flames with... the chamber pot! We never had the luxury of nightclothes, and I remember Mum falling over me as I struggled to put my trousers on to go downstairs. It didn't matter that the bed was on fire, I **had** to put on my trousers before going downstairs.*

My mother would not have holly in the house until Christmas Eve. The reason was, partly anyway, because the year my father died we couldn't afford a Christmas tree, so made do with a holly bough instead.

I tried to help Mum with the housework sometimes, and on one occasion, before she got home from work, I decided to wash the living room floor, which was covered with linoleum and a home-made rag rug. I fetched my bucket of water and got started, but found it very difficult to mop it up; when Mum got home the floor was still swimming in water!

In the 1930s there was a stall on Wellington market which sold ready-made pastry, I think from Trex. Well, I thought I was being helpful one day by trying to make some whilst Mum was at work. Result was that my hands finished up white, and the "pastry" black.

I once pretended to throw a table knife at my sister Mary. The blade came out, and I was left holding the handle. Mum shouted at me and chased me up the yard. But she fell over and hurt her knee, and I can remember standing at a distance but

8

desperately wanting to go and help her. I was crying because I was too frightened to go and help her.

A dear old lady called Mrs Bladen (who lived in the street behind us) made, bottled, and sold non-alcoholic dandelion and burdock. She charged one penny for a bottle.

Occasionally, during the winter, I was sent with a jug, to the Glebe Inn in Glebe Street, Wellington, for a pint of Old Ale. And if any of us had a cold Mum would boil the ale up, adding spices and ginger. Then each of us would have a cup full to make us sweat, thereby getting rid of the cold. Beer was very cheap in those long-ago days. Even when I became old enough to buy it I can recall only paying 10d for a pint.

Sadly, I remember very little about my father; I was only five years old when he passed away from Pneumonia and Malaria. Mary was eight, and David a baby of one year old. I do though remember Dad taking me to work with him one day. He worked at Norah Wellings Toy Factory in Wellington, and I can still picture the enormous (to me as a small boy) teddy bear which stood 'guard' in the entrance!

We were never smacked; Mom's threat of "just you wait till your dad gets home" was enough to keep us in order. If I had misbehaved, I would run up the yard as soon as his bicycle touched the wall of our house.

During his working life, my father served in the armed forces. And it was during his time with the Royal Welsh Fusiliers that he contracted the diseases that eventually killed him. At the time of his twenty-first birthday he was posted in India. He also worked as a plasterer and joiner.

My only other memory of my dad is the day of his funeral. I was left at home with neighbours whilst the service took place. Out of sheer frustration I think, I kicked over a bucket of water which was under the outside tap.

Telephones were extremely rare. I can't think of a single family in our area that had one.

My maternal grandmother, Clara Gray, rented a small and very old cottage in Haygate Road, Wellington, opposite the (then) Brittains Bakery. Later she moved to a new council house; No2 Clift Crescent, Wellington. And some time after she moved there, we left High Street to live with her. It was only a two-up two-down property which I visited recently, and was amazed at how we all somehow managed to live together in that very small house! My uncle Dick Grey lived in Blackpool, and worked as a chauffeur. Sometimes, when his work brought him to our neck of the woods, he would briefly visit us, parking his car (more often than not, a sparkling new American Buick limo) outside his sister's little council house. Also living in Clift Crescent was my mom's sister May with her husband William and their three children.

At about five years of age I started my school life at Prince's Street Infants in Wellington. I have fond memories of my school days. *My favourite subject was English. Whilst I was in the adjoining Junior section of the school my brother David joined the Infants. One day he wrote some rude words in a book, and when challenged about it, he told the teacher that he had learned them from me. I prided myself, however, even at that young age, at not using bad language. Nevertheless, it was suggested that I join the YMCA Boys Club, so I did; and thoroughly enjoyed every single minute of it!*

I attempted, like everyone else my age, the "11plus" exam, but failed. Due to my date of birth, however, I was allowed a second attempt, which I passed. My mum told me later that I was very upset about this because I wanted to go to work, and contribute to our family's meagre budget.

I joined the High School in King Street. The majority of pupils were there because their more affluent parents paid the fees. But I was there by 'Scholarship' as were others, and were looked upon - by some of the richer ones - as 'second rate'. This often resulted in a few scraps, but I was well capable of looking after myself. My love of English followed me to High School and Mr "Dickie" Richardson (my favourite teacher) gave me a love of poetry, and general reading. Memories of him reading such classics as Wind in the Willows *out to the class have stayed with me all my life.*

Life was very difficult for my mother after my father's death. There were no savings. All she had coming in was the ten shillings a week 'Widow's Pension'. The weekly rent for our small house was four shillings, and Mum somehow managed to feed and clothe us all. Later, Mum worked part-time at the Norah Wellings Chad Valley Toy Factory; and when the sugar beet was being lifted and processed, she worked at that local factory too. The work was very hard, but the money helped a lot. It didn't stop us kids worrying though, about our mum shifting two hundred weight pulp sacks day in day out. Hard times; but people didn't moan or complain, they just got on with it; it was a case of having to! Poverty these days just doesn't compare. But we had something much better than money; we had the love and support of our wider family.

Our milk was delivered to our house by a man called Frank Naggington. He had a motorbike and a flatbed sidecar on which he carried his milk churn and measures. One took a jug to him; he then dipped into the churn with his measure, before tipping the milk into your jug.

Some of the "culinary delights" I recall: going to the chip shop in High Street and scrounging batter bits; going to Espleys, the pork butcher for an enormous bag of scratchings, for the princely sum of one penny.

Visits to the doctor were never made unnecessarily; with no NHS, they had to be paid for. But I believe there was an 'unofficial scheme' whereby those who could afford to see the doctor paid a little more (this certainly happened at our doctor's), so the likes of us could have free treatment.

At approximately eight years old I was in the school choir (soprano). I also served as an altar boy at Christ Church, Wellington. I used to roller skate to church; even down the aisle when the church was empty. We earned a few pennies at weddings and funerals, which was good.

When I was ten years old I started to help a man called Freddie Richards on his fruit and veg market stall. Eventually, he acquired a second stall, which I ran totally on my own. My day's pay was one shilling, and as much of the produce (left over) that I could carry. I would also carry home as many boxes as I could for burning on our house fire. On a Saturday Freddie would give me two extra pennies, and let me go early so I could attend the afternoon matinee at the cinema. During the school holidays, and some weekends, I travelled with Freddie in an old Reo Speed Wagon lorry to buy imported produce from the docks at Liverpool. We also went to Pershore Fruit Market in Worcestershire. And actually, on the very day in 1939 when I was about twelve, and war was declared, I was with Freddie Richards at Pershore buying fruit!

Very often I didn't get home till about 10 pm; on Thursdays we had an outside stall, and used paraffin flares to light them. We did most of the markets in Shropshire, and even as far as Welshpool on occasions.

Most of the money I earned went Mum's way, but I did save up and buy my first two-piece suit (short trousers) from Bradley's the Men's Outfitters shop, for ten shillings.

I also got myself an after-school job at Bates and Hunt, the chemist shop. I didn't stick it for long, however. The very first task they gave me was to deliver to a doctor at Redhill, near Oakengates; about three miles uphill. The bike had an enormous carrier on the front, over a small wheel. It was fully laden with packages and large Winchester bottles of medicine. I pushed it all the way because I was terrified of falling over and breaking all the bottles. The return journey was much easier!

At 15 years old I gave up any thoughts of taking exams in order to help Mum, who was still keeping us. My sister Mary had joined the WAAF. I did however get exceptional references which helped me get a position as a Junior Clerk with Great Western ("God's Wonderful") Railway, at Wellington. My pay was fifteen shillings per fortnight. This of course was in the days of steam, and I loved the steam engines. They were fascinating; the steam, the smell, the sound. Even the pride that the various companies, such as the London Midland and Scottish, took in their livery, and the service they provided.

In about 1944/5 I was sent to Peplow station (approximately seven miles down the track) to work as a Porter/Signalman-cum-shunter. I would walk to Wellington station to catch the 7am train to Peplow. One cold winter's morning I was late, and missed the train. I had to walk all the way in the driving snow. Was the Station Master glad to see me? No! As a punishment, he made me unload a wagon full of breeze, then load it onto a lorry for delivery to RAF Shawbury. Just imagine: very small pieces of coal, the size of beans; throwing them over the high side of the wagon with the snow falling, and a strong wind blowing every shovelful back into your face! I didn't miss the train again! And if I had have done, I'd have certainly gone back home.

Hetty was my first serious girlfriend; we married on 29th March 1948 at St Patrick's Catholic Church in Wellington. The priest, Father O'Reilly, was a typical authoritarian. He tried his best to convert me to Catholicism, but unsuccessfully. I did, though, agree that our children could be raised as Roman Catholic. Even this, however, didn't appease him, and he wouldn't allow us to have the choir or church bells, which was very hurtful to both me and Hetty.

We lived with Hett's parents after our marriage, and we were very short of money. But joining the then Shropshire Constabulary on 5th August 1948 came about by sheer chance.

I had previously replied to an advertisement for a position as an Insurance Agent. I waited a fortnight for a reply but nothing came. One day, I was walking in Wellington, and completely on impulse I walked into the police station to see if anything was on offer. I was offered a chance to take the educational exam, which I accepted and passed. That was it! I was now a member of the Constabulary, and was sent to the Police Training Centre at Cannock for thirteen weeks' training.

Of course, two days after joining the police I was offered the

Insurance job. I often wonder how different my life would have been had I not joined the Police Service.

It might be appropriate at this point to say a little about the Shropshire County Constabulary. Shropshire Police Force was created in March 1840, with an establishment of one Chief Constable; six Superintendents, and forty constables. It had jurisdiction for the County, with the exception of Shrewsbury, Ludlow and Bridgnorth. These towns had their own small local police force. Telephones were installed at Wellington, Bridgnorth and Oswestry police stations for the first time on 2nd November 1903; which was also the day that the new county headquarters opened in Shrewsbury. Ludlow and Bridgnorth were amalgamated with the county in 1888, and the last major reorganisation within the force was in April 1947, when the Shrewsbury Borough Force merged with the County.

In 1966 the then Home Secretary Roy Jenkins (Labour) announced that the Shropshire Force was to be included in the biggest Midlands forces merger ever. This move not only applied to the Midlands because the amalgamation of police forces throughout England and Wales reduced the number of police forces from 117 to just 49. At the time of the merger the authorised establishment of the existing Worcester County, Worcester City, Hereford City and Shropshire amounted to 1,477 men and 70 women. The new force strength totalled 1,348 men and 58 women; and so, the West Mercia Constabulary was born!

I was posted back to Wellington at the end of my training. I worked three shifts; mornings, afternoons and nights. Wellington was quite a busy market town even then, but usually there was only one officer in the office and one on the beat. Imagine how many there are these days; and how many of these patrol on foot! No radios back then. Full kit was a whistle, truncheon and handcuffs. Most nights you were out on duty alone. And you had to be at set points at set times, so that you could be contacted if necessary. The reason this was possible and worked well for the most time was I think, due to a fear, and respect of the law.

One of our officers had the grim task of dealing with a horrific road accident involving a pedestrian on the A5, in the early evening. The person killed was a very well respected and noted man in the town. The impact of the vehicle parted the man from his shoes. The body was taken to the mortuary in Walker Street, Wellington. In the lane leading to the mortuary there was a Blacksmith's forge, and some stables.

The policeman involved in this case was only a young man, and was already on the verge of a nervous breakdown; and this was his first fatality. The Superintendent came to the station during the night, and noticed that one of the deceased's shoes was missing from his property. He promptly dispatched the constable to find it. As he walked down the lane to the mortuary in the pitch-black darkness, a white horse poked its head out of the stable, scaring the young officer half to death!

He turned and ran straight back to the police station; and was off work with a nervous breakdown for months!

On occasions I had to visit what was known in those days as a "Common Lodging House", situated in the High Street. The poverty that existed before WW II was extremely grim; and this 'norm' for many people had to be seen to be believed.

Due to the poverty, second-hand shops and pawnshops were commonplace, and well used. I remember a little second-hand shop in High Street. It was run by a Jewish family whose name I can't remember. I do recall though that the daughter's name was Ruth Levi. At this time there was a very strong anti-Jewish attitude in the country. But I got along very well with all of the family.

There was also a Chinese Laundry in the High Street; and stiff shirt collars were fashionable when I was a teenager. The collars were separate from the shirt and one attached them by using a back and front stud. I used to stand and watch the laundry man chew rice, then spit the juice and saliva onto the collars as he ironed them. This practice gave a first class result!

In early 1950 I was transferred to Bridgnorth, and we were given our own police house here. Not a palace by any means; just a semi-detached in need of modernisation, but better than being in digs! We had little or no furniture at first; I can still remember Hett's sister Marjory coming to visit with her baby daughter Janet. And she and Hett breastfeeding the babies on tea chests. Our daughter Ann was born that year.

We bought our first television whilst here, a small black and white one with a 9" screen, and a magnifier. My pay at this time was five pounds five shillings a week, if memory serves.

Bridgnorth was a delightful place to live, and the police could rely on total support from the locals. I learned a lot about life when I lived here.

We had to pull the body of a seven-year-old lad from the River Severn. He had been in there about six weeks. His arm came off as we pulled him out. And rightly, or wrong, we didn't call an ambulance; but quietly took him to the mortuary in the boot of the police car.

My first meeting with the local dentist John Waugh didn't go too well. I wasn't used to visiting a dentist as this was something we just couldn't afford. As I entered his room my first words were: "I'm sorry but I don't like dentists." Quick as a flash, John replied; "And I don't like bloody coppers, now get in that chair." We remained good friends for many years after that.

At a certain pub in Bridgnorth, when you were on duty, you'd go to the back door and ring the bell. Then a pint would appear. If there were two of you, the bell was rung twice; and two pints appeared!

Having a drink in the local hostelry after hours was not uncommon. The landlord was pleased because all the locals had now left. On one occasion however, the landlord kept leaving me for a short while before returning. I couldn't understand this because it was so unusual. I later discovered that whilst I was enjoying a drink in the bar, the Duty Sergeant was supping a pint in the kitchen... and neither of us knew that the other was there!

Hett and I lived on a hill in Bridgnorth Low Town with our daughter Ann. To get to the house required climbing 100 or so steps. And whenever Hett went shopping, which was regular obviously, with Ann in her pram, Hett had to first get down the steps before crossing the river bridge, then push the pram up a very steep hill (The Cartway) to get to High Town. And the reverse on the way back; desperately tiring and very hard work!

It was soon after moving to Bridgnorth that I got involved with helping out at Bridgnorth Boys Club. We ran this fantastic club from a delightful half-timbered building called "Bishop Percy's House".

Then in 1953 I decided to try to reform Bridgnorth Rowing Club (which had been defunct for many years) with the help of a local doctor called Peter Rhodes. We called a public meeting at the Bandon Arms pub, but only about ten people turned up. Nevertheless, we each chipped in half a crown (25p in today's money); thus began the revival. I was appointed Secretary. And during the many years of my membership I have held the posts of Founder; Secretary; Chair; Captain, and Life Member of the

Club. The club has gone from strength to strength, and is now thriving with superb accommodation and boats. Big oaks from little acorns grow!

In 1954 I was posted to Wistanstow (near Craven Arms), South Shropshire, as a Rural Beat Officer. And so began a very different and interesting lifestyle. The police house was situated on the main A49 Hereford to Shrewsbury road, at Grove Bank. And because the M5 and M6 motorways hadn't yet been opened, the traffic along the A49 was very busy with heavy goods vehicles running to and from South Wales to the north of England almost continuously, day and night! At the rear of the house we had a large garden, at the bottom of which ran the railway line. There was also a 'Halt'[1] here which Doctor Beeching closed when he "modernised" the Railway system.

Our water supply came from a well in the yard at the back of the house. The water had to be 'hand-pumped' to the storage tank. Eventually though we did have an electric pump fitted.

My area of responsibility or 'patch' stretched from the boundary of Craven Arms to the Church Stretton boundary. Both Craven Arms and Stretton had its own Police Sergeant and two constables; it was to the Church Stretton Sergeant that I was responsible. I took in all the villages such as Little Stretton; Affcot; Bushmoor; Marshbrook; Cheney Longville, and many others. But most important of my duties was the A49. Fatal

---

[1] A 'halt' on the UK railways is a request stop, smaller than a normal station, where the train will only stop when the driver or guard has been asked to do so.

accidents were common, and when they happened, which was all too common, you were on your own! The Lazy Trout cafe, between Marshbrook and Little Stretton, was always very busy with lorry drivers (and their bosses who arrived at all hours to pay them off); and also numerous local "ladies of the night" plying their "trade".

To patrol my beat, I used a 150cc BSA Bantam motorcycle, eventually upgrading to an Ariel Leader 205cc. This bike was fitted with a radio so for the first time in my career I was in contact with Headquarters.

As time moved on I became involved on a voluntary basis with numerous groups and organisations in and around our little village. And I have to say, my wife Hetty was more than tolerant with me spending so much time helping out wherever and whenever I could, being the full time local "bobby" an' all! She accepted, and encouraged me in everything I did.

My time in Wistanstow was among the best years of my life!

In 1956 my wife and I got to hear about the 'Women's Voluntary Service' (as it was called then; and later the 'Women's Royal Voluntary Service'). They were apparently operating a holiday scheme for "under-privileged" children (from the urban districts of Wolverhampton and Birmingham) to stay in country houses in Shropshire. Hetty and I took an eight-year-old girl into our house for a fortnight's holiday.

This was successful, so the following year we had a young boy stay with us. And again, this was very successful. Then in 1958 we progressed to having a couple of boys at our police house. These lads had the idea that camping in a tent in the garden would be good fun; and it proved to be so. This gave me an idea, and as things turned out, one of the most important ideas of my whole life! It also made me think about the number of lads, probably hundreds, who had never had a holiday from the humdrum of their everyday lives. And the more I thought about this, the more determined I became, to try and do something about it, with Hett's valued help and approval.

Having the children stay with us over the previous couple of years brought me into contact with a truly fantastic lady. Mrs 'Robin' Hazlerigg, who lived at Ryton, near Dorrington, was the local Holiday Organiser for the (then) WVS. She worked tirelessly for the benefit of the children, and played a very active and important part in the success of my annual Camps. Her energy, positivity and vitality became a constant; I was very grateful for her ongoing support.

We both felt there was a need, or at least a desire, to increase the number of children whom the WVS could provide a holiday for. So I began to look around for a suitable site with the facilities required to run a camping holiday for about twenty or so lads.

My neighbouring beat bobby Bill Newbound (of Aston on Clun), his wife Miriam, and myself got together to discuss the possibilities of obtaining some tents, and finding a place to run a Camp. I cannot now recall where exactly the tents came from but we did manage to acquire one or two ex-army ridge tents.

Bill and I were both involved in the Shropshire Association of Youth Clubs, and together we ran the first and second Camps in 1959 and 1960 in a field on Minton Oaks Farm (which was on my police beat) by kind permission of Mr and Mrs D O Jones. On that field stood a rather ancient corrugated iron Nissen hut, which had a simple dirt floor. The cooking was done on scrounged Calor gas cookers; the borrowed tents were erected around the hut. The majority of my staff were only youngsters themselves, and were members of the Youth Clubs that Bill and I were running. Both Camps were a brilliant success, and this pleased Robin as much as it did myself and Bill.

By 1961 both Bill Newbound and I were running our own voluntary Youth Clubs in our respective villages; and very much involved with the Duke of Edinburgh Award Scheme. To this end we acquired, through the kind generosity of a local landowner, the temporary use of a somewhat derelict cottage at Hammonds Green, near Craven Arms. And with his approval, we used the cottage as a kitchen, and a staffroom; erecting the tents in the adjoining field. We had previously "christened" the building 'Endeavour Cottage', having used it for some Outward Bound courses for our Youth Club members prior to my third WVS Camp.

For this year's Camp we had no sleeping bags. But palliasse covers, ground sheets and blankets (supplied by the WVS, and

Shropshire County Council Children's Department) proved more than sufficient.

In 1962 we were back on David Jones's land, but this year we camped on a field just inside the entrance to Minton Batch. Roy and Di Williams again, as last year, cooked for us. Perhaps it is fitting for me at this point to mention the vast amount of work and organisation that went into arranging and operating each ten-day Camp. I could not possibly have done it without the solid support of so many people who in their own individual way, did everything they could to help me succeed. I thank them all, from the bottom of my heart.

In 1963 another derelict cottage came to our rescue! This time though, it was near Picklescott, a village on the Long Mynd. It was owned by a Mr Ross, who very kindly allowed us use of the cottage and the adjoining field. I have always loved the Long Mynd, and therefore I was delighted to be back there with my Camps.

And in 1964 we found a field that served us well for the next sixteen years; thanks to the kind generosity of Mr Jack Williams of Minton Farm, and his lovely family.

We set up Camp initially on the western side of the brook which meandered through the field, but from 1965 (Alan Scriven's first year at Camp aged 12yrs), we moved across stream to the part of the field that will be forever associated with the WVS/Longmynd Adventure Camp.

I tried to purchase the field, even though I had no idea where *the money was coming from; it was more than adequate and ideal for us. Jack, however, gave me a polite refusal, but very kindly 'rented' us the field for our Camps at a very acceptable peppercorn fee of five shillings per annum. And that fee was never once increased by Jack or his son-in-law Ted Challinor.*

We managed to purchase our own site during the late seventies, and our first Camp on this field took place in 1980. I missed the 1979 Camps through ill health. Alan Scriven took my place at the helm. I made him my official 'number two' in 1980; and as a way of thanking him for stepping in at such short notice, I invited him to join the committee in 1981.

I have been able, during my life, to be involved with a good number of charities and organisations of which I am happy and proud.

But starting "The Camp" from the rear garden of my Police House in 1958 (having joined the Force on a whim) is, I believe, my finest achievement. And I offer my sincere thanks to everyone who assisted me down the years, in whatever way they could, but most especially, to my wife Hetty; and my daughters Ann and Debbie. God bless.

Humble Beginnings

At the time of the Camp's inception I was a five-year-old lad living in poverty, with four siblings and our mother. We shared a three-bed council house in Fifth Avenue, Low Hill, Wolverhampton, in South Staffordshire (as it was back then). My home town, oops... 'city', is now part of the West Midlands. I mentioned in my first book that the Royal Hospital proves that Wolverhampton was part of South Staffs. I could have included the old South Staffordshire Regiment building on the corner of Thornley Street and Stafford Street in the now city centre.

I was the middle child, having a brother and sister above and below me (Michelle arrived in 1966). Our family was surviving, just about, on weekly National Assistance (the term for Government Benefit before 'Social Security' was introduced) hand-outs, and Family Allowance. During the early sixties our mother managed to find herself a part-time evening job as a cleaner at the *Express and Star* newspaper premises in Queen Street. Our eldest sister, Pat, was left to look after us all, and she did a good job, bless her. But for now, it was just National Assistance. We were told, and had no reason to question it, that our dad had been killed whilst cycling to work on the A449 Stafford Road one foggy morning. There was therefore no 'father figure' for us kids to look up to; but our mother more than made up for this.

After the six-week summer break in 1958, I moved from the school's nursery to join my brother Billy at Woden Road Infants. And I have to say, I enjoyed (almost) every minute of my school life, which took me, finally, to Springfield Secondary Modern, after my six years or so at Woden Infants and Junior Schools. My "education" (I use the term lightly) steadily improved as the years rolled on; but I left school in 1968 with not one single qualification to my name. The option to stay on and continue my education was offered by the school headmaster, Mr Beddoes. I had to refuse his kind gesture, however, because Mom needed me to start working in order to contribute to the family budget.

As a five-year-old, I had no concept or understanding of the struggle our mother faced on a daily basis as she tried to provide for us. She received a modicum of assistance, now and again, from the Education Authorities with our school uniforms; and we were allowed free dinners at school (which saved her a massive five shillings per week for each one of us in full-time education). But that was the limit regarding government assistance.

About a year before I started nursery school, my sister Pat, my brothers Billy and David, and I were put into the Cottage Homes, a local children's home. My mother told me years later that the reason for this was to give her some temporary relief from the stresses and strains of trying to raise a family on her own. Our sister Carmel, just a year old at the time, stayed with Mom. We weren't in there very long - just a couple of weeks (some kids more unfortunate than us lived their whole childhood in this dreary old 'institution') - but it was long enough for me to remember the experience to this day. The Cottage Homes was situated in Amos Lane, Wednesfield, Wolverhampton. My siblings and I all shared one double bed in a tiny room.

One night, as I remember vividly, my sister rolled over, and pushed me out of bed! It was very dark and I became a bit frightened so I decided to go and find someone to help me get back onto the high bed, as I couldn't seem to manage it myself. Slowly, I felt my way round the bed, edging towards the door. Opening it with some difficulty, because I had to reach up and turn the large white doorknob, I found myself on the landing. As I pulled the door closed behind me, I accidentally caught the bottom of the white night-shirt I had been given between the door and frame, tearing it slightly whilst trying to free it, and myself, without the struggle of opening the damned door again!

Eventually, I began to very slowly descend the stairs. I could hear voices behind the door at the foot of the staircase. I was very scared by now; thinking all the time (which seemed like hours) until I reached the bottom that I would at the very least be severely told off for my little escapade. As things turned out, I couldn't have been more wrong.

I tentatively reached up and grabbed the cold white doorknob, and slowly twisted it. I knew from the voices that a man and a woman were on the other side of the door. It creaked loudly as I pushed it; the voices fell silent, and I started to cry as I made my awkward entrance into the room, and their space. The lady; a very old (to me) but kindly soul, dressed like an old-fashioned nurse, rose from the big armchair beside a roaring fire and walked quickly towards me. The man muttered something I didn't understand before breezing past me and out of the room, into the corridor.

'Hello my love,' the old lady said soothingly. 'Can't you settle?'

I blurted out something along the lines of: 'My sister's pushed me out of bed.' This caused the lady to chuckle as she picked me up and carried me to the armchair, where she plonked me down.

'You sit here and don't move; I won't be long. And keep away from the fire.'

I didn't budge. She returned in almost no time with a small cup full of warm milk; and a little piece of ginger cake. I'll never forget the taste of that, it was sharp and bitty... but I ate it all the same!

The old lady spoke gently as I gulped the milk down, saying she would take me back upstairs and make sure I was alright; which she did.

Each time I saw that dear old soul during the remainder of the time I was resident in the Cottage Homes, she always had a smile and a kind word for me.

But any mention of the Cottage Homes as I was growing up put "the fear of God" into my siblings and our friends in Fifth Avenue. It was made out by the grown-ups to be a real dark, sadistic place where no good came to any child unfortunate enough to be sent there... "If you don't behave, I'll have you put in the Cottage Homes" was a constant threat to us all. But I held no fear of the place.

During the winter months of my early childhood years it seemed to snow heavily every year! We would return home from school to a tasty and filling stew Mom would make from odds and ends, plus a cheap breast of lamb, or maybe the occasional rabbit from a good-natured friend who sometimes went shooting along the canal bank. When I got a little older I used to go on "shooting expeditions" with this kind family friend called Jesse Ball, known to everyone in the neighbourhood as JB. He was a good man, was JB. Sadly, he was fatally injured after falling under the rear wheel of a moving JCB digger. He had been sweet on my mom but although she wasn't interested in that way they got along pretty well just as friends.

***

While this was going on in Wolverhampton, over in Shropshire, after several lengthy discussions with Hetty, Bill had decided

31

that he could accommodate a small handful of boys in his rear garden. As mentioned by Bill, they had already had some success with taking in children for a holiday. A tent was all he needed, and that soon arrived. The next thing to do was decide how many lads he could invite, then work out how to bring his plan to fruition. So after again contacting Mrs G. M. Hazlerigg (WVS Children's Holiday Organiser) at her office in Shrewsbury, Bill agreed on a "small handful" of lads to stay with him and his family.

His mission was accomplished. The lads thoroughly enjoyed the short break from their humdrum lives back home. Bill was, naturally, very happy with the success of his kind offer to welcome a small number of young strangers into his family and on the day of their departure he was as proud as any man could be of what he had achieved with the unbending support of his good wife Hetty.

Bill's daughter Ann was just eight years old at this time so therefore has very little recall of the lads who shared the family house and garden all those years ago. Something she does remember, however, is an incident with Gerald (the first lad ever to be given a holiday at the Police House, in 1957) and a grass snake!

A photograph of Gerald (taken in the rear garden with Bonny, the family's pet golden retriever), which Ann still treasures, shows him as a very smart young man in his early teenage years. He's posing for the picture in jacket and trousers, white shirt with a patterned tie, and a V-neck pullover tucked into his trousers. He even has a handkerchief popping out of his top pocket. Very dapper! To round off Gerald's excellent appearance (considering his probable social circumstance), he is wearing spectacles. His hair, which he looks to have plenty of, is very neatly parted.

As Ann recalls, she and Gerald were playing in a small copse beside the house when they chanced upon a grass snake. A couple of minutes later, Ann was very suddenly (in her own words) "put off teenage boys" after Gerald decided it would be fun to put the snake down a drain! That day had a strong and lasting effect on the young Annie because it was an incident that she remembers vividly to this day.

Delighted by the success of Bill's first ever venture into caring for a few socially deprived young lads, Robin Hazlerigg wasted no time in asking if he would consider doing it again the following year, as (Robin told him) there were any number of boys in the same position as those who had taken that first holiday at the Police House. Mrs Hazlerigg said she felt sure that she and her colleagues in Wolverhampton and Birmingham would be able to raise sufficient sponsorship for perhaps a dozen or so lads to benefit next year **should** Bill be in a position to do it again. As things transpired, Bill accepted responsibility for twenty boys on a borrowed field.

The ball was now well and truly rolling...

Family Heartache

My maternal grandmother was found dead in her bed on 4th January 1958. For a good while before her death, she had been confined to her single bed, which stood in a corner of our living room, nearest the open fire. My sister Pat found her on that cold winter's morning. I remember my mom's younger sister Emma arriving with a few of my cousins (Emma had a large family) to help Mom with the arrangements that had to be made when a person died. Emma was a truly great lady who I loved almost as much as I loved my mom and the two sisters were very close; inseparable, almost. My siblings and I therefore spent a lot of time with our nearest cousins during those early years of my childhood, which was wonderful because we all got along really well. My favourite cousin, growing up, was Emma's eldest son, Harold. I looked up to him, as I still do; 'H', as he was known to us all, was always great fun to be with. I missed him a lot after he joined the army. One day, though, he surprised us by rolling up to our house with a few of his soldier colleagues, on board a tank!

Emma and her husband Harold were as poor as we were because he hadn't worked for a while so their family were also dependent on National Assistance. The two sisters were the very best of friends always. They loaned small amounts of money to each other when they could, and shared what food they had when money was regularly out of the question.

When I was around ten years old my mom gave me a five-pound note (the first one I had ever seen) and asked me to take it to Emma. My aunt and her family lived in Kipling Road, Fordhouses, which was about a half-hour walk away. When I arrived at Emma's, I discovered to my horror that I had lost the money! My aunt, bless her, was very cool and calm. She just said, 'Never mind, son, you didn't mean it, accidents happen, go home and tell your mom.' Easier said than done!

I started the journey home feeling very anxious. I was well aware, as we all were, of the importance of looking after what bit of money we had. And five pounds in the very early sixties was a massive sum of cash to most families, not just the ones who shared the same boat as us. I had visions of my mom going absolutely bananas at me. I'd definitely be grounded for a while, and my siblings would tell everyone what an idiot I was. I started crying as I trudged along Showell Road, putting one foot in front of the other whilst dreading arriving back home! And then I saw it...

There, skidding along the pavement towards me, was a ten-pound note! I was absolutely and totally transformed; over the moon; delighted; ecstatic. But more than anything, I was relieved. Relieved that our two families wouldn't have nothing to eat until the next Family Allowance pay day; or the next National Assistance hand-out; or my sister Pat's next wage packet from the Ever-Ready factory... or the few quid Mom and us kids earned for picking potatoes (or "tater pickin'"[2] as it was referred to back in the day). My sister's wages didn't help us for long because she left home almost as soon as she began to earn.

I ran the remainder of the way home and, as I tried to catch my breath, told my mom the whole story. I wasn't afraid now to tell her about initially losing the fiver. But I should have been! She gave me a massive telling off before sending me and Billy back to Emma's with seven pounds and ten shillings after she had carted us all (except Pat) up to Showell Circus shops ('the Circle' as us locals knew it) to change the note.

I had no idea why my mom would be giving Emma such a vast amount of money, or where it had come from. And it was more than my life was worth to ask. You just didn't! That's how it was in those days.

Sadly, however, Emma was to die in April 1964, at the young age of thirty-nine. And this unfortunately caused a "parting of the ways" for our families, at least for a while, until our cousin

---

[2] During the school summer holidays many of the women in our neighbourhood went potato-picking to earn a little extra cash. And it was almost always the case that if your mother went picking, be it potatoes or fruit, you went with her... and you picked as well! We were collected by an old short flat-bed lorry with sides and a tailgate, which offered at least a little safety as the driver went about his rounds picking families up and then carting us all off to the farm. The farm we usually went to was Pugh's, in Albrighton. Occasionally, we would be picked up by a bus, and ferried to a farm in Pattingham. But whichever farm we went to, the routine was the same. The women would have a ridge, and their kids - the ones deemed old enough to work - would be given half a ridge to pick the potatoes from. The smaller children would simply play around in the field with the women working together to keep an eye on all of them. It was back-breaking work, and at the end of the day you had thoroughly deserved your money... most of which went straight into your mom's purse.

Lenny joined my brothers and me at Camp later in the decade. Our Lenny was also destined to live a very short life. He had followed our 'H' into the army, and was a serving soldier home on leave when he met with an accident on the Cannock Road near Wolverhampton town centre. He was just twenty-one years old.

***

The success of Bill's initial foray into giving a few poor urban kids a break in the deep countryside of South Shropshire led to annual Camps being held on a number of fields not too far from the Police House. Every year, Bill gave up ten days of his annual leave from the police force so as to enable him to run the Camps.

The article below appeared in the *Shropshire Star* in August 1959, shortly after the very first Camp; and I am very grateful to Shropshire Newspapers Ltd for kindly allowing me to include it, and some of the following articles in this book:

PC Gave up Holiday to Run Boys' Camp

It's a good job that Wistanstow Police Constable William F Williams, and his wife Hetty, love children. A few more mouths to feed... even at short notice... never bothered them. Not even at ten o' clock at night!

It was only a few days after Mr Williams had given up ten days of his fortnight's annual holiday to run a Camp for twenty boys from the Midlands that a knock came at the door of his home.

Outside was one of the 'holiday youngsters' with two of his pals, who had hitch-hiked from their Wolverhampton homes to visit the Camp leader. "They'd left home at 2pm and had planned to return again that same night. But it was then 10pm, so we gave them a meal and decided to put them up for the night," says Mr Williams.

But the family however, already had one extra guest - Janet Clarke, their nine-year-old niece, who was fast asleep upstairs with their daughter Ann, also nine. "We had to move the girls into another room to make way for the boys."

Since the holiday, Mr Williams has received eight "thank you" letters, and two telephone calls from the boys, and he has invited a few of them to his Police House home for a weekend in September.

The camping holiday – under canvas at Mr D O Jones's Minton Oaks Farm at the foot of the Long Mynd – was the first (proper) one that Wistanstow Youth Club Leader Mr Williams had led, in conjunction with the Shropshire WVS Children's Holiday Scheme.

Cooks at that very first Camp were Mrs Miriam Newbound, the wife of Aston-on-Clun Police Constable Newbound (co-leader of the village youth club), and eighteen-year-old Heather Perkins of Little Brampton. Some of Mr Williams's club members; Tony Price and David Maund; and Ludlow Grammar School boys Richard Edwards and John Price (both aged 15) helped to run the Camp.

A head-and-shoulders picture of Bill accompanied the report.

Below is a short article which was published in the local *Advertiser* a few days after the lads returned home on Friday 14th August 1959:

This week in the Advertiser *Office we have been taking off our hats to acknowledge a very nice gesture by a certain village constable. PC Bill Williams of Wistanstow could have been on annual leave with his family at Blackpool or Brighton, but instead he forfeited part of his holiday to make sure that 20 young boys, less fortunate than he, could have their annual holiday. The boys are from some of the poorer homes of Birmingham and on Wednesday (August 5) they arrived at Minton Oak, Marshbrook, to spend 10 days under canvas. The holiday was arranged by the Birmingham and Shrewsbury branches of the WVS and PC Williams and some of the boys of Wistanstow Youth Club are camping with them to organise the holiday programme. We wish them a very good stay.*

What a lovely article (except for the fact of no mention of Wolverhampton WVS; but that's just me being biased perhaps)!

So we're off!

From humble beginnings, the "WVS Boys Camp" was now up and running. And from my own humble start, I too was beginning to find my path in the life and family I had been born into.

Growing "Pains"

With Mrs Hazlerigg's unswerving devotion to helping Bill make a success of his original idea, the WVS Boys Camp began to prosper; in a manner of speaking.

The number of lads selected from (mainly) Wolverhampton and Birmingham to enjoy the experience of camping in deepest South Shropshire increased slightly each year; and the number of people ready and willing to volunteer their help to Bill on the Camps was also on the up. It was, however, still a case of having to borrow everything that was needed to stock a campsite, even down to the portable toilets!

The Wolverhampton coach company Don Everall Travel Ltd was the chosen transport for the beneficiaries. The driver would initially go to a pick-up point in Birmingham where the 'Brummie' lads waited with unbridled excitement, whether they had been to Camp previously or were leaving home for the first time. And, once safely boarded along with a WVS lady escort, the coach would set off for Faulkland Street, Wolverhampton, where the driver would complete the loading of his precious cargo. A lady escort, usually Mrs Marjorie Lathe from the Wolverhampton WVS Office (which at that time was in Broad Street, before later relocating to Fryer Street), would board last, along with Mrs Winnie Hull – also WVS – who had volunteered to cook for Bill's Camp. And whilst the coach made its journey slowly west, Bill Williams and his staff, consisting of work colleagues and friends – many known to him from Wistanstow Youth Club – would be busy making the site, wherever it happened to be on any particular year, fit for purpose... theoretically, at least.

I say this because during the very early years Bill accepted any and every form of help regarding items he considered a necessity.

Just prior to the arrival of the coach, Bill gave his customary talk to the helpers on how the Camp would be operated with regard to programme, discipline, staff responsibilities to their group of lads, and the ongoing tidiness of the campsite. This was always most important to Bill because the campsite (wherever it was until 1980) was on borrowed land, therefore it was vital to maintain the condition it had been in before the Camp was set up.

The programme of events remained fairly constant throughout the Camp's first forty years. The games we played (as mentioned in my first book) inside and outside, depending on the weather, were brilliant. So too, although we didn't always appreciate it, were the long walks over the magnificent Longmynd. We all learned so much about the hill, and Shropshire's fascinating history, from our Skipper.

Seaside day (usually on the Wednesday) began in earnest and

the excitement just grew and grew for all the lads, the vast majority of whom would be seeing the sea for the first time, unless of course they had been lucky enough to be on their second, third or even fourth holiday at Camp.

The local press continued its interest in the Camp; the following article, written by Gordon Riley, was published in the *Shropshire Star* whilst Camp 1960 was still rolling along:

Simply Great

When I was a lad, the standard formula for angry parents went something like this: "I'll fetch a policeman to you..." And somehow, that gentleman of the law became a big bad bogeyman in blue.

Fortunately for me, times have changed. Journalism has its compensation in that personal respect. But one wonders, with all this talk about juvenile delinquency, whether they have changed for enough people.

The bogeyman technique was alright years ago perhaps. In this different age, maybe, a new approach is needed.

I think Bill Williams, 34yrs old village constable at Wistanstow in South Shropshire - although perhaps shrinks from admitting it - may well be on the right track in crime prevention.

I went yesterday to the Longmynd Camp at Minton Oak near Church Stretton. Officially, it is the WVS Boys Camp for children who would not otherwise get a holiday. It is for boys whose fathers or mothers are dead; children of large families where parents are weighed down perhaps by the cares of life and the economic struggle.

Leader of this Camp, for the second year running is "Williams the law" (as I gather he is known on his beat). He is guide and mentor to 38 boys aged between ten and fourteen years inclusive from Wolverhampton, Dudley and Birmingham. In the delightful surroundings of "Little Switzerland" under canvas and thoroughly enjoying the outdoor life, many of the children are having their first experience away from home; and thoroughly enjoying it too.

Also, for the lads, it is a chance to meet the law in a new guise.

Gives up His Leave

Bill is a native of Wellington. Before he went to Wistanstow he was stationed at Bridgnorth. And for the second year running he has given up 10 days of his 17 days' annual leave, to lead these lads. And just imagine a policeman sitting in a thorn bush bound and gagged, playing games with his charges!

He founded the Wistanstow Youth Club, and still leads it.

Bill started these Camps by originally taking a child into his home under the WVS Holiday Scheme.

This is a sacrifice not only by Bill, but also for his wife Hetty and their ten-year-old daughter Ann.

"My wife has always encouraged and supported me in this

work," he comments, "If she didn't I should never have been able to do it."

Bill enjoys the Camps as much as the lads. And twelve of the boys from last year wrote to him; four are still in touch. One boy from Wolverhampton has even found his way to the Police House in Wistanstow several times, by cycling... and even hiking!

It's Not All Fun

Yet it is not all fun in Camp for Bill. The night before I met him, he had spent the small hours caring for one of the boys who had a recurrence of a foot injury. This meant getting the local doctor out of bed, and also Mr David Jones who provides the land for Bill to hold his Camps.

But it's all worthwhile. On Sunday, Bill took 28 boys to church; every one of them making their own choice whether to go along or not.

He isn't the only one at Camp, obviously. Bill also has a school teacher from Kent helping him; as well as two student teachers, and three members of Wistanstow Youth Club.

The visits to church did, however, become a thing of the past towards the end of the sixties, initially due to logistical problems. But Bill made up for it by conducting a short and simple "service" of sorts, which was suitable for all Christian faiths.

Growing "Pains"

The Camp, as stated by Bill, would be held wherever permission could be obtained. From 1964 and for the next fifteen years, however, it settled in a beautiful spot in Minton, near Church Stretton.

***

As the Camps rolled steadily on towards my first ever holiday there (or anywhere), in 1965, I was getting on with my life as best as I could under the stresses and strains of poverty.

There was no uniform requirement at Woden Road Junior School so Mom dressed us as smartly as she could afford. I can't remember ever receiving new clothes that hadn't arrived courtesy of the WVS; 'make do' was the order of the day for all of us so borrowing each other's clothes as and when was a real necessity. Truth to tell, though, this "system" did cause some patches of trouble between us brothers. It was different for Pat and Carmel due to the nine-year age difference; and Michelle didn't arrive until just before England enjoyed its first and only World Cup Football win.

During the winter months, when it was very cold, we would be given a pair of old socks to wear as gloves; we never had more than one coat, and our shoes had to last! When I was about nine years old there was a period when I didn't have a proper pair of shoes to my name. My mother solved this problem by removing the studs from a pair of brown leather football boots

I had been given. I even had to wear them for school for about a fortnight! The mickey-taking was extreme as I remember, but we were a very poor family so any footwear was a bonus, regardless.

There were times when Mom could have easily given us up, but the thought never crossed her mind. She struggled on with a determination that nothing and no-one could break. Some nights, after we had been sent to bed, Billy, David and I would hear our mom crying. Never once, though, did we dare to go downstairs to ask her why. Partly because we knew it would cause her extreme embarrassment; but also because there was no doubt she would have hit the roof! Bed meant bed; end of!

Years later, I plucked up the courage to ask our mom why she cried at night. She put her head down and said very softly: 'Because I didn't know how I was going to feed you all the next day.' But she always managed to do it... somehow.

Most of the children at school took some lunch, which would be consumed during the morning break along with the small bottle of milk we all received daily. That was a luxury our budget could never run to. Breakfast was either porridge, or five "morning coffee" biscuits, and a piece of bread toasted on the open fire if Mom could afford to light it so early. If not, it was placed over a gas ring on the stove in our "back kitchen", and that meal had to last us until dinner time at school. We had free dinners.

There was hardly ever a sufficient supply of cups and crockery to go round so we improvised again by using jam jars for cups. And when plates and dishes were scarce, we 'made do' by using one or two of the saucepans Mom had used to cook the meal in. Our mother had to cook everything from scratch, and whatever she was able to purchase had to last. I can remember being sent up to 'the circle' shops to buy a repair kit for our saucepan(s) when they began to leak. You could also get broken biscuits from Warrilows, the hardware shop; my brother Billy was possibly their best customer for these. He would collect empty beer bottles from here, there and everywhere then take them to the Bushbury Arms pub in Showell Circus where one could exchange them for a few coppers each. Billy's "profits" were always spent on broken biscuits. The pub landlords got wise to the 'bottle returns' caper... well, the bottles that were nicked from the pub grounds, and taken back again for more money. They came up with the novel idea of stamping the labels of the bottles that were returned, so they couldn't be brought back to the pub for another pay-out.

When hunger caught up with us, which happened regularly when we were out playing football – either in the street or over the field behind our house – my brothers and me and a few of our friends walked down to the chip shop at the bottom of Fifth Avenue. Upon arrival, one of us would go inside and politely ask if there were any spare batter bits! We were hardly ever refused a small bag of bits, which we would share amongst the group.

On one or two occasions, if we were extremely lucky, the man or lady serving would put a few chips in the mix for us.

There was also the greengrocer's shop in Hawksford Crescent, towards the bottom of our street. In there we would "beg" for bruised fruit. And, as with the chippie, we were more often than not obliged.

My years at Woden Road Junior School passed into my life history in July 1964. I enjoyed all four years of my time at this wonderful school. The teachers (with the exception of Miss George) were always very nice to us and Mr Hull, our headmaster, was a real joy. My friendship with Kenny Turner had developed into us being proper best friends – and this has continued throughout our lives – both inside and outside school. We don't live in each other's pockets but our friendship has been solid and constant; never forgetting each other at Christmastime and birthdays.

An amusing incident (though not so for me at the time) involving Kenny and me happened when we were both about eighteen years old. He was working for the National Tyre Service in Gorsebrook Road, Wolverhampton as a mobile tyre-fitter. Ken had the use of a small pick-up during business hours. On the day in question I was at home taking it easy after my day's work at Carvers, the builders merchants in town. Kenny called at our house and I went to the door. He was very excited as he asked me to go with him to put some fuel in the pick-up so that we could use it later that evening. I asked him how he came to have the vehicle after work. He told me that as his immediate boss had asked him to refuel it after working hours he could go home in it and drive it into work the next morning.

'Hang on a bit then, mate,' I said, 'I'll just go and put my shoes on.'

'Oh don't bother, Al, you're going to be in the cab, you won't need them, mate. Come on, because I've got to go home after and get changed before I come back for you.'

'What do you need me for, mate? You go and fill up, then go and get sorted, and then come back for me.'

Now that suggestion, I thought, made better sense. But my mate wasn't having it. I think he perhaps wanted to show off his driving skills to me... again!

We arrived at the petrol station on the Stafford Road, where the National Tyre Service had an account. Kenny got out of the cab to re-fuel the motor. At the precise moment that he replaced the nozzle, a car swept in to the fuel station and drove straight at us, stopping just short of our rear bumper. I did think about getting out and telling the driver what I thought about his erratic driving but remembered that I had nothing on my feet, and would therefore look a right fool. Instead, I leaned across the cab and looked at the man through the rear-view mirror. A short and quiet conversation between him and Kenny took place before Ken got back in the cab.

'Fuckin' hell, mate, you ain't gonna believe this,' Kenny said, shaking his head and looking straight at me.

'What's up Ken, who **is** that twat? Tell him to piss off, or shall I?'

'It's the gaffer, Al, the big boss. And he's just told me I've got to take this fuckin' thing back to our place right now.'

You can imagine what was racing through my mind!

'Bloody nora, mate!' I shouted. 'You'll have to take me home first.'

'I can't mate, soz. He said he's following me back to the yard, right now.'

'Fuck sake.'

'You'll have to get out here, Al, and I'll meet you at the top of Gorsebrook Road in a minute.'

'I can't, you daft twat, I've got fuck-all on me feet, or hadn't you noticed!'

With this, my best friend just fell about, laughing. But I wasn't laughing, not right then! I had no option but to vacate the vehicle because Ken's boss came right up to the passenger door and opened it. Then he tilted, or flicked, his head whilst looking me directly in the eye. I didn't wait for an invitation as I awkwardly got out and walked off in the direction of the Bridge pub, on the Stafford Road, opposite Gorsebrook Road. Kenny started the engine and swung off the forecourt. I watched as he turned left, then I crossed the busy road to wait for him. It seemed like hours before he came walking, nay, almost crawling, towards me... he was laughing so much. That 'episode' still ranks amongst the most embarrassing events of my life to date. Walking all the way back home to Fifth Avenue, absolutely bare-footed, and Kenny taking the piss every inch of the way!

As the school year of 1964 came to an end in July, my brother Billy completed his first year at Springfield Road Secondary Modern. He was now beginning to get excited, and a little nervous, about leaving us, for ten whole days! He had been selected, Mom told us, by the local Women's Voluntary Service for a place at some holiday camp in Shropshire, wherever that was! I was glad they hadn't picked me as well. The mere thought of leaving my mom horrified me. It didn't matter where this place was, or how much fun could be had (according to the WVS lady, Mrs Lathe, who visited our home to inform Mom about the offer of Billy's inclusion in this year's holiday); I wasn't interested.

The day arrived for him to go off on this 'mystery tour'. He was a little apprehensive but he didn't moan or cling to Mom's apron as I had when I was eight years old and had to be admitted into the Royal Hospital. My mom and I had been asked to sit in a corridor after registration, to wait for whoever was to come and fetch me. Soon, a nurse appeared and introduced herself to us both before taking my hand with the intention of separating me from my mother, in order to take me to the children's ward. I wasn't having it! With my other hand I grabbed hold of my mom's coat and gripped it with every ounce of strength I could muster. I was screaming, crying, and begging Mom not to let this woman take me, all at the same time. It was a fruitless effort. Soon I was in a small ward for very young children, off one of the men's wards. I settled down eventually, and spent five long days in the place. All's well that ends well...

The Camp Billy attended in 1964 was blessed with great weather, and a happy and capable group of men (as well as Mrs Hull), who gave their all to ensure every one of the boys had a good and memorable holiday. Needless to say, when my brother returned to us he couldn't shut up about the place. He said it was fantastic and brilliant; great fun every day, and he hoped he would be allowed to go again next year.

By the time my turn arrived, however, Billy had completely changed his tune. Now, apparently, it was the worse place on earth... but why? Because of our argument over the television, as described in the first book! Billy didn't want to make things easy for me.

While he was away having this apparently great experience, David and I spent most days with our friends from the street and nearby, including Kenny, getting up to stuff kids of our day got up to. This included playing football in the street, as well as non-ball games such as British Bulldog, Postman's Knock, and Kick the Can. Some of us, including me, were also starting to take an interest in the local girls. I was always friendly with the girls living near me, especially Christine Fieldhouse who lived next door. I liked her a lot but she always kept me at arm's length. Kenny's sister Ann was a girl I got to know from visiting his "neck of the woods" on some evenings. She too, though, kept her distance a little. I am still friends with Ann today but lost contact with Christine as we grew up and each of us kids from Fifth Avenue went our own way.

We lads loved to go to the local tip during school holidays; to us it was a wonderful place, at the top of Leacroft Avenue, at the other side of the junction with Sandy Lane. We would just mooch about, looking for stuff of interest (to us) that the good people of the borough had binned. And if we had a couple of coppers we could spend them at the little shop where the number three bus turned round at the end of its route.

The bike park at the top of Fifth Avenue was also a place of fantastic fun for us. One could hire a bike for two pennies, which secured half an hour's ride. But we would always stretch it (especially if we had no more money) by ignoring the old man whose job it was to hire out and call in the bikes on a P.A. system that had seen (and heard) better days, as had most of the bikes! Everyone had their favourite, so it was a bit of a disappointment if the bike you fancied was already out when you went in search of it, having paid the old man and got your precious ticket. There were lots of occasions when we would fall off our bikes, especially just after we'd learned to ride the damn things! And a bruise or two would be the result if and when we tried to impress our mates by taking out a bike that was obviously too big for us. I learned to ride a bicycle on the very same day as my cousin Mary. She was a few years my senior but hadn't yet grasped the art of it; or, more probably, hadn't had the chance. On the day of our joint success, our two families were spending a warm summer afternoon at the park, which also had all the amenities of an ordinary kids' park, so there was fun for everyone at that great place.

The 1964 summer break from school, however, was destined to be my final one without the inclusion of an annual visit to Camp.

New Experiences

I joined Billy at Springfield Secondary Modern School in September 1964; approximately a month or so after he returned from his first camping holiday.

I was allocated, thankfully, with Kenny, to Form 1b, which was the middle class. Once we were settled into our new form room, we were all divided up into four groups: Drake, Grenville, Frobisher and Raleigh. I have absolutely no idea of the reason for this, but each group had its own colour. I was placed in Grenville, so my colour for the whole of my time at the school, for all events such as Sports Day, PE and the like, was red. Drake wore blue (I wanted to be in Drake because blue is, and always has been, my favourite colour); Frobisher wore yellow, and Raleigh sported green, if my memory serves correctly.

Being very interested in British (and later, American) history, I did some research on our group names and discovered that Sir Richard Grenville was a British Naval Commander at some point in the 16th century. In fact, all four were British seamen during this period of time in our history. Sir Walter Raleigh was an explorer, and a 'favourite' of Queen Elizabeth I, while Sir Francis Drake held the titles of Vice-Admiral, and English Sea Captain. I also discovered that (strangely) Sir Martin Frobisher was listed as an English Seaman; and a "licensed pirate".

I can't recall our group ever enjoying success but at least "our man Grenville" was a Commander!

By the time I reached my third year at this great school I, along with Kenny, had progressed to 3a, with our final year being spent in 4a.

Although I left with no qualifications, I "excelled" somewhat in my favourite subjects, English and history, according to my annual school reports:

End of term, July 1965: Number in Form (class 1b) 29. Form Position 9th.
English 7th: History 6th.
Form Master's comments: Alan has shown that he can work well, but frequent absences may have stopped much more success.
Headmaster's comments: A very poor attendance record has affected his work.
Absences: 64
Conduct: Good average.

End of Term, July 1966: Number in Form (class 2b) 30 Form Position 4th.
English 1st: History 5th.
Form Master's comments: Excellent exam results. Alan is a pleasant boy who is developing a sense of responsibility. He could take a bigger pride in his appearance however. A very

good final position; well done.

Headmaster's comments: Good. He has worked well.

Absences: 29

Conduct: Excellent.

End of Term, July 1967: *Number in Form (class 3a) 28 Form Position 7th.*

English 1st: History 4th.

Form Master's comments: Very able. Alan is a very willing boy and a pleasant one. Generally keeps himself as tidy as possible. Good class position.

Headmaster's comments: A good report; he has worked well.

Absences: 56

Conduct: Very good.

End of Term July 1968: *Number in Form (class 4a) 24 Form Position 18th.*

English 10th: History 7th.

Form Master's comments: A fairly satisfactory Report. Alan has been away from school at times due to illness. A very poor examination result in English, surprisingly. He has made steady progress though, with no special effort being made.

Headmaster's comments: Quite good progress, except for two very moderate exam results. Alan is pleasant and reliable.

Absences: 21

Conduct: Good.

I think, overall, my school reports were diabolical! And without attempting to make excuses for myself, I have to say that very poor attendance in two of my four years at Springfield contributed, without doubt.

The reason for my poor attendance record was, in the main, a health issue with my stomach. I have suffered on and off all of my life with stomach trouble. And being a member of a very poor family, who could only afford to eat the cheapest of everything, obviously didn't help.

My appearance is also mentioned a couple of times in my school reports. This bears out the fact that I was a child of poor standing; living in poverty with my mother and siblings. We never had new clothing; it was always a case of the WVS helping to clothe us, and whatever Mom could pick up cheaply from the various jumble sales she attended regularly.

***

During the four years I attended senior school, the Camp became an important part of my life. It's no secret that I hated the place initially, but I quickly grew to love it, so much so that during the winter months between my holidays there, I could think of almost nothing else. And by the time I left school I had become a very junior member of Bill Williams' voluntary staff. I had also begun to spend the odd weekend at Bill's home in Shrawardine, Shrewsbury.

One of the tent leaders when I was a boy was a young man called Mick Powell. Mick, a native of Craven Arms, knew Police Constable Bill Williams very well from Wistanstow Youth Club, where he was a member. Mick offered his help at the fledgling WVS Boys Camp of 1964 and Bill was delighted to accept, although Mick was only about a couple of years older than some of the boys. He was great at Camp; always happy and enthusiastic about everything. It was sad for Mick and the Camp when his time as a helper came to an abrupt end after the 1971 Camp. He went and got himself married, and that was the last I saw or heard of him... for just over forty-five years!

I am very happy that Mick is now back in my life and one of a small number of people I consider a true friend. And it pleases me no end to say that he has lost none of the infectious joviality and good nature that so endeared him to everyone at Camp during those long-gone halcyon days.

Mick surprised me recently. He told me that when Bill realised I shouldn't be at Camp in 1968[3] he called a short meeting of sorts with a couple of members of his field staff, including Mick and my tent leader Pete Roberts (whom I am also delighted to be re-acquainted with now) to ask their advice on his idea of making me a (junior) member of staff for the time remaining.

---

[3] Readers of my first book will know that I had passed the "Insurance limit" of fourteen years of age by the time I was at Camp 1968. Bill Williams cottoned on to this fact halfway through my holiday but rather than send me home, he made me a junior member of staff and the rest, as they say, is history. At least my history!

That was very decent of the Skipper; he could have just sent me packing. I think, however, that if he'd opted to do that, my thirty years as a voluntary staff member would probably never have happened, because I might not have thought about offering my help. And I don't mean that in a vindictive or spiteful manner.

Neither Bill, nor any of the staff, ever told me anything of this, but I am very grateful to all of them; especially Bill.

The following words belong to Pete Roberts. They are his response to my request for information regarding how he came to be one of Bill's helpers:

I joined the Shropshire Police Cadets in September 1967; at that time Bill was the village 'bobby' at Wistanstow.

In October of that year I took part in the first Longmynd Hike, representing 26th Shrewsbury Scouts. And on 1st October 1967 Shropshire Police Force amalgamated with Herefordshire, Worcestershire and Worcester City Forces, to become 'West Mercia Constabulary'. The Police 'powers that be' decided they wanted to get the force noticed, so it was decided to enter a West Mercia Cadet team to take part in the 1968 Hike. It was at this time that I first met Bill, as he was designated to assist in our training, because his local knowledge was "second to none".

His character was amazing! And although he didn't actually walk with us, he ensured that all our night stops were in the outbuildings of public houses situated in the area. In those days we worked hard and played hard!

Our team came first in the hike, and this was certainly a feather in Bill's cap. During those days I got to know Bill very well; and this was when he told me about the WRVS Camp at Minton. Bill arranged with our bosses for myself and one or two other cadets to assist at the Camp as it would - he said - assist us in gaining some local knowledge, and perhaps help us with our fitness for future Longmynd Hikes.

Bill had the "gift of the gab" in a nice way; therefore I quickly became involved with his Camp at Minton, and loved it! So much so that I was a member of his tent staff for the next few years, sometimes helping on both Camps each year. And I've never believed that he had me there 'for my holidays'!!!

That was Bill, though. You would do anything for him. He was that sort of man.

The Camps were operated without too much consideration for "health and safety" or "political correctness". It was all down to Bill, and good old common sense! There were times prior to the Camps when Bill would meet me at Minton, and we'd carry out various repair jobs. Invariably, we would end up at one of the local pubs until the early hours. There was never a dull moment with Bill.

Bill and I stayed friends and remained in contact right to the end; always reminiscing about Camps of long ago; and our *nights around the Campfire with a few bottles after the lads had settled down. And the 'ritual' of putting the fire out before we retired ourselves.*

Bill was a "character" throughout his life; he knew everybody, and everywhere. Every problem he had was solved quickly, because he knew who to ask, or where to go for whatever he needed. It mattered not whether these people were rogues or pillars of the community. Bill had the charisma to "get things done".

What a brilliant tribute to a truly amazing man!

Pete Roberts himself had a very noticeable presence at Camp, aided by his fit, wiry frame; he was also a very popular tent leader. Pete was greatly missed by all of us "regulars" at Camp when, due to personal and work commitments, he had to cease his valued involvement. Even so, he stands out in my list of best helpers throughout my three decades-plus with the Camp. And I am proud to say that Pete was one of my tent leaders during my years as a beneficiary of that magical place.

At the end of the 1960 Camp Bill had a brilliant idea which certainly stood the test of time. On the final day of the boys' holiday, he displayed his and all the staff's addresses on a makeshift notice board, inviting the lads to write to anyone they cared to after returning home. Sadly, only one letter from that

Camp survives. It was written by a lad called Tommy (no surname given), from Wolverhampton, on 3rd March 1961. In his short correspondence Tommy offers the briefest hint of what life was like for him at home:

Dear Skip

I am sorry I have not written to you before now but I have been very busy. Are your family in good health? How is Helen? [I don't know who Helen was; perhaps he was referring to Bill's daughter Ann.]

I have got a bit of a cold, otherwise I am alright. Mom sends her thanks for the jeans you gave me. She said I looked a proper mess in those others. By the way Skip, I'm sorry I left that other pair behind, please do what you want with them. Or leave them till I come again and I will bring them back with me. Well that's all for now. Take care of yourself.

Write soon.

Tommy.

A note at the top of the page tells us that Bill replied on 17th Oct 1961. Over more than three decades, Bill received, and replied to, hundreds of letters from the boys. I used to berate him gently for the time it took him to reply to mine but when I began to receive mail from the lads myself, it quickly became evident how difficult it was to reply to the many letters sent year on year. I can't recall, however, having to wait seven months, as Tommy must have done!

Correspondence between the lads and the Skipper; the lads and the staff, and the staff and the Skipper (and between the staff themselves) was as much the 'life blood' of the Camp as anything else that made it so successful. I know Bill loved receiving the letters. When I became his trusted number two, he would regularly call me to his caravan, sometimes offering me a small aperitif before getting out an A4 folder which was full of letters, mainly from the children. Bill liked to read them to me, and he would do all the voices and actions he thought the writer was trying to get across; brilliant! On most occasions, the boys failed to see the importance of dating their letters. Therefore, many of the selection I have chosen to include will be dateless. The content, however, will help to date some of them.[4]

Bill was delighted to receive the following letter, penned on 30th August 1962, from one Tom Badger, of Heath Town, Wolverhampton:

Dear Mr Williams
Thank you for the lovely holiday you gave us. I enjoyed it very

---

[4] It would be nice to be able to return these letters to their creators. Therefore, if anyone reading this book is the writer of a letter I include, and would like to have it returned, as I have already done with some, you can find my contact details at the end of the book.

much. *If you should meet Mr (David) Maund or any other helpers who live in Craven Arms, will you please thank them too. Today Mrs Russell (WVS) came to visit us, and she told me she had met you.*

Next Monday I am going away to a boarding Grammar School. It is the Queen Elizabeth Grammar School in Ashbourne, Derbyshire. I will probably write to you again before next year when I hope to be seeing you again.

Yours truthfully

T R Badger

Bill replied on 11th September 1962... truthfully!

A little earlier, on 14th August 1962, Trevor Halloran wrote a beautiful letter to Bill, which I couldn't resist including. Trevor was a Birmingham lad, from Ladywood:

Dear Sir

I hope you are alright. I got home safe and sound. The weather is very, very bad today. It has been thundering and lightning. I would like to know if you could send me the addresses of the other helpers because I would like to write to them too.

I liked the orange, and crisps that the cooks gave us when we got on the coach. We arrived home at half past twelve. My nan met me and John, to take us home. I hope you get all the criminals in the town. I hope all your family are alright; and you too.

Me and my brother John would like to come next year to the camp. And thank you for the prize at the campfire for Best Cook. I have read up to page 32. I will soon finish the book so I will buy another book of the same series. I think you are the best policeman in the county. I will have to stop now because I want to go to sleep tonight. So goodnight, hope to see you again soon.

Your Camper
Trevor Halloran

I wanted to include the above because it says so much, about Camp, and about Trevor himself.

Trevor tells us that he won a book prize; an 'Observer' book. Bill always gave these out as prizes (for various achievements) at the Campfire. He believed in these books; considered them very educational (and they were) so therefore an excellent prize, well worth winning. I still treasure the copy I won for Best Camper in 1967.

The pop and crisps were a regular occurrence on the coach trip home. The poor driver must have spent a good while cleaning the seats and floor after we had been set down at our dropping-off points. We were also given pop and crisps on our journeys to and from the seaside.

Another competition worth winning, if you fancied getting your hands on an Observer book, was the Best Magazine Article.

The very first edition of the Camp magazine was produced in coalition with Wistanstow Youth Club's *Country Endeavour*. The only article worth a mention here, however, is a somewhat gruesome account of the origins of police constable Bill Williams' Wistanstow village:

Headline News...........1114 Years Ago

It is ridiculous to assume that anyone, speeding along the main highway and seeing the village sign-post could imagine any historical detail. After all, what do they see? A few peculiarly coloured cottages among which is a police station and an unprepossessing mound of red-brick which vaguely resembles a product of Sammy Morelands factory.

Yet behind this chiaroscuro facade lies a romantic story. Probably the most interesting detail tells of the inauguration of the title "Wistanstow", or anciently "Wystanstowe". The name is attributed to St Wistan, a Saxon saint, the grandson and heir of Wizlaf, king of Mercia, who was treacherously murdered in the village in A.D. 849, by his cousin Brithford. Thomas de Marleburge, Abbot of Evesham described this event in his "Chronica Abbotiae de Evesham":

'A council was assembled at a place known from that day to this as Wistanstowe in Shropshire, and to it came Bartulph and his son Brithford. Under his cloak, Brithford concealed a sword and while giving Wistan a kiss of peace, struck him in the head, and gave him a mortal wound.'

The body was taken to Derbyshire and was buried in Repton Abbey. 'But for thirty days a column of light extending from the spot where he was slain to the heavens above, was seen by all who dwelt there. And every year, on the day of his martyrdom, the hairs of his head severed by the sword sprang up like grass.'

A church, St Wistan's, was erected on this spot to which pilgrims made their way each year to see the miraculous growth of hair. Unfortunately, no trace is left of that church. But the present church stands on the exact site - built between 1180 and 1200 with a fourteenth century tower.

The article is attributed to 'A.B.D.L.', whom I consider a worthy winner.

Fascinating stuff, especially if one is interested in knowing the alleged origins of such a pleasant English village. And South Shropshire is abundantly blessed with these beautiful places; every one of them worth a visit.

Wistanstow parish church, Holy Trinity, provided the venue for the Memorial Service of Bill Williams BEM. It took place on Monday 28th October 2013. The church, as expected, was packed to the gunnels with family, friends and colleagues from Bill's life and working career. I attended, accompanied by friends of mine and Bill's who had helped him and me (as Bosun) during his years at the helm of the charity he created.

New Experiences

A poem read from the pulpit, perhaps summed Bill (and his way of life) up better than any other words could have:

If I should die and leave you for a while
Be not like others sore undone
Who keep long vigils by the silent dust and weep.
For my sake, turn again to life and smile.
Nerving thy heart and trembling hand to do
Something to comfort weaker hearts than thine.
Complete these dear unfinished tasks of mine,
And I perchance may therein comfort you.

Mary Lee Hall

Also in the congregation were three sound and reliable volunteers from the sixties and seventies: Pete Roberts and Mick Powell, and Richard Lewis, who went on to become an Anglican bishop.

It was a sad day for obvious reasons, but at the same time, it was good to have the opportunity to rekindle old friendships, which hopefully will lead to new beginnings.

Steady Progress

Readers of my first book may recall that one of the programme favourites at Camp was the Ghost Hunt. Briefly, the 'ghost story' tells the tale of two lovers who meet their end on a bridge in Minton Batch in mediaeval times. Their names were Lady Lucy Lamplight and Sir Buckley Minton-Beddoes.

I have no idea where these 'people' originated from except to say that our Skipper introduced them to us by way of his very convincing story (told in its entirety in my first book) about unrequited love and a subsequent gruesome event. The strange thing about all this, however, is that one tent leader on the 1964 Camp was a chap called Buckley Minton-Beddoes! Buckley was present when I first went to Camp the following year. I remember him as a tall, slim and pleasant sort of bloke but in 1964 he managed to engage the wrath of the future Bishop Richard Lewis. My third-hand knowledge of this altercation is that Buckley and Richard had a disagreement of sorts, resulting in Buckley squaring up to Richard, who wasn't much smaller than Buckley in height... but several pounds heavier, apparently! I'm not sure that Buckley was a 'man of the cloth' himself, despite living at the time at the Vicarage in Lydbury North, South Shropshire; but Richard definitely was! So what was the outcome?

Well, Richard kept his cool, saying the matter could and would be sorted later, when both had had the opportunity of calming down. This was a very mature response indeed. The following morning, however, Richard went looking for Buckley and suggested that the two of them go off into the next field, away from prying eyes, and settle the matter once and for all. Off they went. A couple of minutes later, Richard reappeared on the Camp field. When asked by the Skipper where Buckley was, Richard calmly replied, 'Oh, he'll be back, Skip, when he wakes up.' Or words to that effect!

Only 28 lads made up the 1964 Camp and of those there were six sets of brothers. Brothers were always given the choice to stay together, or to separate into different tent groups. Invariably, though, as in my case with Billy and David, brothers stuck together. In 1964 Billy shared Tent Three with Graham Russell, Nigel and Nicholas Ordinans, and a certain John Preece, who readers of my first book will know all about. Peter Williams, son of the "infamous Butcher" took charge of this group.

My late brother submitted the following, for the magazine:

My Bonny flies over the ocean, my Bonny flies over the sea.
My Bonny flies into my dreamtime; I do hope she'll come back
to me.

Just a simple little 'ditty' but a contribution all the same; and that was all that was asked of us. During the 1960s we all looked forward to receiving our magazine. It was a fantastic reminder of where we had been and what we had done, which was nothing like we would do year-round at home.

I felt that Tom Badger's tongue-twister was also worthy of inclusion:

An imaginary menagerie manager imagined that he managed an imaginary menagerie. But the imaginary menagerie he imagined he managed; was the imaginary menagerie his manager managed.

And this, by John Brace:

Definitions
SUCCESSION..............Baby's feeding time.
BIGAMIST.................Larger Mist.
ETHICS....................A county north of Thuthex.

Both lads were members of Tent Four, led by Mr BMB.

***

In 1965 my chance to sample this wonderful and remarkable place at "the back of beyond" finally arrived!

Steady Progress

The year began with me as an eleven-year-old boy living in Fifth Avenue, Low Hill, Wolverhampton. It wasn't difficult to know how much pressure our mother was under on a daily basis, to keep us fed and clothed as best as she could. Our house was very basic with regards to furniture. I can't remember it being re-decorated more than once and that was only the sitting room. We had some red flowery wallpaper given to us and our mom, bless her, did as good a job as she could to cover the walls with it.

It was about this time that she met a man I will, for the purpose of this book, refer to as "JJ". He was lodging with a family who lived further down the road, on the same side as us, but it seemed like no time at all before he had moved into our house. And how our lives changed as a result! He was an okay bloke but soon took it upon himself to become "man of the house". JJ suggested we should call him "Dad". I had absolutely no intention whatsoever of complying with this suggestion and I told him so to his face, at eleven years of age!

His response was, 'Well, we'll see about this. I'll have a word with your mother. I'm here now as her partner.'

'You might be her partner, but that doesn't make you our dad,' I replied.

A couple of hours later, when we all went home after being out with our friends in the street, JJ was nowhere to be seen. I asked Mom if he'd left. 'No, he hasn't left,' she answered, quite abruptly, 'he's gone down the Corner House [one of the local pubs] and when he gets back, or from tomorrow, you'll call him Dad.'

'I won't, Mom,' I replied. And I never did! And as far as I can remember, none of the others did either, except for Michelle, and we all accepted that. To her, JJ *was* her dad.

Our eldest sister left home almost immediately after JJ moved in. She quickly married her boyfriend, Leslie. I liked Les very much. He would take me to the Molineux, the Wolves stadium. He also took me to quite a few away games, even though I kept telling him I supported Manchester United. He wouldn't have it. But being with Les made me feel wonderful, and grown up. On match days we would meet his twin brother Malcolm, and half a dozen of their mates, in the Elephant and Castle pub at the top of the Cannock Road, near to the Molineux. Les used to sneak me half a pint of bitter when the landlady, Mrs Davies, hadn't got her beady eye on me!

We were in the Barley Mow at the bottom of Lower Stafford Street one night when I was still under-age. Les put a pint of bitter in front of me and said, 'Get that down yer, bruv.' It looked massive! I thought I would never be able to drink all that; it was the first pint I ever had. I told Les, but he just said, 'Bollocks, drink it, you'll love it.' And I did 'love it', eventually. But I was looking for excuses not to.

'Hey Les, that old woman over there keeps looking at me,' I said, hoping he would take the drink away from me. All I got in response was: 'She's probably wondering why it's taking you so bloody long to drink that pint. Come on, don't show yourself up.'

My late brother-in-law Leslie Jones was a great bloke, and I respected him a lot. I made steady progress growing into puberty with his help, guidance and enthusiasm.

The Longmynd Adventure Camp also made good, steady progress throughout the sixties.

The Camp had a major effect on most of the lads who were lucky enough to be selected; not least myself. The letters below offer a couple of differing examples:

Dear Mr Williams

Thank you for a good holiday. My mom said you are a good man giving up your holidays for 30 camp boys. Thank the cooks for cooking our meals in the time we was there.

I am sending you a picture of me on another camp. But it is not better than your camp. Please send it back.

Thank any helpers if you see anyone. Goodbye for now Skipper.

No name given. But this letter was written on 14th August 1962 from 44 Alexandra Street, Ladywood, Birmingham. The following was written to Bill on 24th April 1964 from Oldswinford Hospital School:

Dear Skip

This year unfortunately I have not been put on the list for your camp, due to a mix-up at home. But I would be very pleased if I could come along with a friend. I will bring my own tent (two-man), sleeping and cooking equipment, and food. My friend is very enthusiastic about camping, but his parents won't allow him to go camping unless he is with a group. I am sure he will be a great help about the camp.

Yours faithfully,

Charles Gunter.

During my years with the Camp, one or two issues arose regarding lads having extra holidays, usually at the seaside, as well as coming to Camp. Some members of staff, upon discovering from the child that he had been on a previous holiday, or was going on another holiday after Camp, were a bit put-out. They didn't understand the concept of selection, and considered that the child had no right to be at Camp if his family could afford to take him away themselves. Bill, however, always had the same answer once the matter(s) reached his ears. He simply pointed out that no-one amongst us, bar himself (and me, later) knew anything of the child's personal circumstances, so shouldn't waste their time worrying that the lad was stopping another child perhaps more worthy of having a holiday at Camp. And besides, Bill said, maybe the child was "romancing" a little to hide what was really going on at home.

One child, however, was telling the truth about having a holiday at the seaside **but** he missed out on coming to Camp in doing so:

To Skip
I hope that the ghost hunt went well, as well as the campfire. I am having a great time. (Unreadable) said I can come to the camp next year, and I would be very happy to come.
David Hirst.

This was from a postcard sent from Bournemouth on 23rd August 1982.

Bill received a "case history" on each child. He read them only if he thought there was a need to do so, for instance if something occurred involving a child and he considered that learning a little more about the youngster might help to resolve the situation. I agreed with this, and employed the same policy when I became Skipper. All the documents were destroyed immediately after the children began their journey home.

I learned that in a lot of cases children, including myself and my brothers, were sent to Camp in order to give the parent(s) – if there were any – a short break from the pressures, worries and responsibilities of their offspring. And occasionally Bill received a letter of thanks from a grateful parent. This very touching example came from a mother in 1967:

Dear Mr Williams

I would like to take this opportunity to thank you and all the helpers for making my son's holiday so enjoyable.

I am very proud of him. He works as a grocery boy, and even when he only has a few coppers (in tips) he offers them to me. And he always puts ten shillings in my hand on a Saturday.

I am a widow, and have two other younger children, who went together to a farm in Stafford. It is the first holiday they have had, and they all had a wonderful time, all due to kind people like you, and not forgetting the WVS.

It is twenty-two years since I have had a holiday, but I was at least able to have a rest, knowing that my children were happy and in good company. They are even talking about next year. I know David said he wants to come back to see you and the other leaders.

So once again, thank you all for all your good work.

I remain Sincerely

Dave's mother.

Saltley, Birmingham 8

So the Camp was definitely making steady progress. And so were the final evening Campfires, so brilliantly conducted by our Skipper.

Below are a few excerpts of Pat Hazlehurst's observations of 'Minton Camp 1968':

To be invited to the Campfire at Minton is a privilege. And to be so privileged has been my happy lot for the past six years. Each year I think, 'Well it can never be as enjoyable again,' but when the next year comes along, I am always proved wrong...

I find a particular joy in bringing along new visitors, and watching their reactions to another wonderful finale to what I know is always a very enjoyable week for the 'campers' and helpers alike...

The good spirit so evident has been built up throughout the week, and surely the fire itself has taken the week to build too...

At about 8:30pm the campfire was lit as we all took our places around it. Before the proceedings were officially started by the Skipper, the boys spontaneously began singing; it was very obvious that they had all had plenty of singing practice during the week...

It is impossible to mention all the very good acts, ditties, and personal performances that were put on for our pleasure; the prize for the best one, however, was won by Tony Page of Tent One...

The Campfire finale is always a very moving occurrence. It starts with the prize-giving for all achievements during the ten-day Camp. And then the Skipper brings the proceedings to an end with a short prayer of thanks for yet another successful Camp...

We left the Camp at about eleven o' clock with our bodies

warmed by the hot soup served from Mrs Hull's kitchen; and our hearts warmed by the wonderful spirit of friendship always in evidence at Minton Camp.

Pat Hazlehurst was a Camp stalwart from the very early sixties, until her death in 1996, aged 83 years.

When the coach arrived on the morning following the Campfire Pat was writing about, in 1968, I was beset with an awful feeling that this was it. My short time with this brilliant place was over!

Yes, the Skipper had very kindly allowed me to stay for the duration after telling me on Sports Day that, being fifteen, I should not be there, but now here I was, ready to board the coach home for what I thought would be the last time. I so envied all the lads younger than me, because they would have the chance to come again.

The Skipper grabbed my right hand as I put my foot on the bottom step of the coach. 'Thanks for all your help since Sports Day, Alan, I really appreciate it,' he said quietly. The tears began to well up, and soon my vision became blurred. I had to take my chance NOW!

'Skip, do you think I could come as a helper next year, please? I don't want this to be the end for me. I'll work hard for you, I promise.' It was verging on begging.

'We'll see Alan, we'll see.' And with that, the man who I was now looking up to as the main male influence on my young life let go of my hand and turned to the next lad who was waiting to board the coach. I held myself together as I found a seat next to my brother David. He too was probably (I thought) seeing the Camp for the last time, but he was in good spirits; looking forward to going home to Mom, actually. It must have played on his mind a little, though, because I found the following letter amongst some correspondence Bill gave me shortly after I started to write my first book:

Dear Skipper

I had a wonderful time at camp, and I wish I can come next year. I hope you and your family are alright and well.

Thank you for those wonderful books you gave us for winning the camp competition (the best tent group throughout the duration) they're good books to read.

Alan started work on Tuesday. Really I wish I was still at camp because I don't do much at home only watch television and play outside.

If I can come next year I will only come as a helper, not one of the boys, because I really think you need help at camp.

We didn't play all the games we should have played at camp this year Skip; Cowboys and Indians for instance. The Sports day by the way was good this year; it was a better standard of people playing. The cross country race was run especially good. Although I came second, I shouldn't have come second really because I had hurt my foot, and Mr Gausden told me to rest it for a while, but I didn't.

It was the best holiday I have had in the time that I have been coming to camp, thank you.

Well Skipper I can't think of much else to say at the moment, but I will write again soon. Please write back won't you. Goodbye for now, signing off.

Yours Goodly

David Scriven.

My brother gave his address as 16 Camp Street (long since eaten up by the University – much like the former Carvers premises, where my working life began). This was the home of my sister Pat and her young family. Why David was staying there is a mystery to me although truth to tell, all of us brothers stayed with our eldest and dearest sister at some point. She never refused and neither did Leslie, despite having six kids themselves, a couple of whom also came to Camp!

My own first correspondence of 1968 to Bill Williams, soon after my seemingly final holiday, wasn't as lively and upbeat as David's:

Dear Skipper

I hope this is not too early to write to you. I just wanted to tell you that we all got home alright.

Thank you very much indeed for everything you have done for me throughout the four years that the WVS allowed me to come to camp. I will always be grateful to them, and to the helpers, but most of all Skip'; to you. You are a truly great man and I will be very sad if I don't come to camp again. I have started working at Carvers in town as a warehouse assistant. It's okay but the money is no good, it's a job though I suppose.

If you feel that I can be of use to you as a young helper, like I was after you told me I was too old to be at camp as a boy, I would love to do that. And I promise to work hard and do as I am told. But it is your decision Skipper.

Enclosed is a photograph of me which I hope you won't mind me sending to you.

Take care of yourself, and reply in your own time please.

Bye for now

Alan Scriven.

Bill replied almost immediately, thanking me again for my help; and promising to let me know "later" about my offer of help. Thankfully, he kept his promise, replying positively during the spring of 1969.

The letter (below) was written to Bill Williams on 19th Aug 1969. I have selected this as the final piece for this chapter. It offers thanks to our Skipper for the holiday enjoyed; and also pays a glowing tribute to the lad's twenty-year-old tent leader, Mick Powell.

Dear Mr Bill Williams

I'm so glad you had invited me to stay at the camp for ten days. Thank you for the food that we had.

Will you write back to say that we did see a ghost because my mom doesn't believe me. You were the best at the camp, out of all the staff; then the second best was Mr Powell. In the pictures Mr Powell bought everyone an Aero who was in tent two.

When we went ghost hunting my knees were trembling with fright. One of the ghosts was about ten feet high.

Your loving friend

Andrew Buxton

Andrew lived in Shirley, Solihull. His wonderful letter was swiftly replied to by Bill, on 28th August 1969.

I went to Camp in 1969 as a junior helper, and I thoroughly enjoyed my one and only Camp as the 'gofer'. For the 1970 Camp, I was asked to be a tent leader. My own steady progress was now fully underway.

The Super Seventies

The 1970s began for me with progression at work. I was now a member of the trade counter staff at Carvers, but nursing other ambitions. Whilst in my final year at school the English and Drama teacher, Mr Kingston, had suggested I should consider drama school when I left. He had arrived at this idea after watching me perform in the various school plays. I played Bassanio in *The Merchant of Venice*; remembering always my second line in Act One, which is a promise I have tried to honour throughout my life:

"I will not fail you."

In *Twelfth Night* I took the part of the comic character Sir Andrew Aguecheek. I was also selected by Mr K to take the Bible reading at morning assembly on a number of occasions because, he said, I was a very good speaker. This was to serve me well in later life when I would be required to make speeches, or give talks about, the Longmynd Adventure Camp.

I also had dreams of making it as a footballer, but my own stupid and immature behaviour put paid to that!

A career in the armed forces appealed to me for a while but I had somehow found myself taking a position as a warehouse boy at Carvers. The reason undoubtedly was the fact that after my school days were over my mom needed me to work and contribute to the family budget, as my brother Billy had been doing for almost a year. I've got absolutely no regrets about the road my life has taken; I believe in fate and everything happening for a reason. The police force also took my fancy after I met Bill Williams. But I just kept plodding on (no pun intended) at Carvers.

Some weekends in my middle teens were spent with my then-girlfriend Tina's family. I was invited to join them on trips to Birmingham for visits to her dad Patrick Harte's Irish relatives. I loved these weekends. On every occasion, Tina's mother would pre-warn me that the "Irish lot" were "rough and ready" and I might hear the occasional swear word. I didn't mind that, and they couldn't be any more rough and ready than my own family!

Whenever we rocked up at their place, which was a different address on almost every visit, we were made very welcome immediately. There was always lots of food and drink; then in the evening we would all go to either a pub or the "Busmen's club" for a fantastic night of old-fashioned karaoke. These fabulous sessions were called "free and easy evenings", with an open mic and a sole pianist.

The very first time I went with the family to Birmingham will stick with me always. When we arrived, everyone – all but the family matriarch, Pat's mother Isabella – was gathered in the kitchen. I stuck close to Tina, as there was a massive mongrel dog lurking about the place. I wasn't keen on dogs since being bitten by an Alsatian one morning during my paper round.

I was assured that this pet of Tina's family was "lovely" and "wouldn't hurt a flea". Slowly but surely everyone, including Tina, made their way into the sitting room. I didn't want to appear cheeky (I've always known my place) so I stayed in the kitchen. Big mistake! As soon as I was the only one left, that bloody dog went for me with earnest! I fought it off, however, until the cavalry arrived in the shape of Jimmy, Tina's uncle.

'He won't fuckin' hurt yer,' said Jimmy in his strong Southern Irish accent, as the bloody thing dragged me round the kitchen!

The other incident I'll remember forever involved Tina's cousin Annette, and the Harte family matriarch.

Unbeknown to me, Annette, who I suppose would have been about fourteen or so, sidled up to her grandmother, pointed me out and said, 'Nana, that's our Tina's boyfriend. He's a fuckin' wanker.'

A short while later, Annette came to me and said, 'The nana wants to meet you, Alan. Come with me.' I followed her across the room to where Mrs Harte Senior was sitting in an old but very comfortable-looking armchair.

'This is Tina's boyfriend, Nana, what is he?'

The old lady turned her head very slowly towards me; looked me up and down, and said, 'He's a fuckun wankor.'

Annette almost wet herself laughing!

I absolutely loved our trips to Birmingham.

The year 1970 was very special for me. I was excited but at the same time a little nervous upon my arrival at that beautiful field we called home for a few short days each year. I was going to be looking after a small group of young boys for the most part of their holiday at Camp. I say 'most part' because there were times, of course, when all the lads came together under the direct care and authority of the Skipper. In 1970, Bill's hands were a little bit tied due to one or two people not showing up to help after having promised their support. I was, therefore, thrown in at the deep end. But I got stuck into the task and, with the valued help and support of other leaders who were by now "seasoned campaigners", I managed to do a worthwhile job. My group included the Simpkiss brothers: Jimmy, Terry and Tommy. What a great bunch of lads they were. Always happy to take part in whatever we were doing, either as our own little group or with all tent group games and activities off-site.

The Skipper told me, on the final morning of Camp 1970, as he was allocating jobs to the volunteers who had remained on site after the boys' departure, that he was very pleased with my "contribution" and would like to see me back next year. I was over the moon! Here I was; a young helper who had been a beneficiary of this man's ongoing wonderful act of kindness for four great years, now helping to strike Camp after my very first experience as a fully blooded member of staff.

Initially, I was to travel back with the boys on the coach but Bill kindly offered to run me home. I like to think it wasn't just because he was shorthanded.

My first ever letter of thanks for my help as a tent leader came from the WRVS, written on 22nd August 1970:

Dear Alan

I would like to thank you for your splendid help that you gave to the Camp. I must say that I did appreciate your vitality at the Campfire.

Skip tells me that you have been a jolly good leader. I hope that you enjoyed it and that you will be able to come again.

Yours sincerely

G M (Robin) Hazlerigg

WRVS County Staff

The first correspondence from Bill, however, didn't arrive until early January 1971. He first of all thanks me for my "two or three" letters since Camp 1970, before going on to tell me his reasons for "making me wait", as he put it.

Bill was off work due to high blood pressure, and hadn't felt much like doing anything. He said this letter to me was the first he had written since Camp. This made me feel very special, and valued as one of his troop. He continues by saying how much he appreciated my help, then offers me another invitation to stay at his house (by this time the family were living at Shrawardine in Shrewsbury, Salop):

Perhaps when the weather improves a bit you can come over to see us. I'd like to see you and talk Camp. It doesn't really matter when, as long as I'm off duty.

I did go and stay with Bill and the family in April that same year. I was accompanied by my friend and fellow camper, Terry Hogg. As I said in my first book, Terry helped out at Camp for a couple of years after reaching fifteen years of age but then disappeared forever as far as helping at Camp was concerned.

My time with Carvers of Wolverhampton was thoroughly enjoyable and I was happy and contented with life as the middle of the decade approached. Sadly, this wasn't to last.

I married Tina in 1974, at which point in my working career I was Warehouse Manager, earning a pittance of a salary. Carvers was always well-known in the building and plumbing merchant industry for below-average wages. In 1976, shortly before the birth of our first child, Marc, I left to join Ward Bros Ltd (mainly a plumbers' merchant company) as a telephone salesman. I hated it. The immobility of the job finally got the better of me and I quit the company after twelve months.

Tina and I were by this time living in a council flat on the sixth floor of a tower block, in Portobello, Willenhall. We were both working full-time although at Marc's arrival Tina stopped working for a short time. Once our boy was 'out of the woods' after his premature birth, Tina went back to work and my mother looked after Marc all day every weekday; we couldn't have managed without her. I would catch the bus into town with Marc and Mom would be waiting at the bus station. Then it was a very quick 'transfer of responsibility' for the baby, after which we went our separate ways before meeting up again at the end of my working day. Mom was brilliant. Nothing was too much trouble for her and Marc loved being with her.

This arrangement continued until 1978, when we were offered a council house in Bushbury. By this time I had a car so it was easy for me to take Marc to my mom's and collect him after work. Jenks and Cattell Ltd, the garden tool manufacturers, were now my employers. I began, thanks to my father-in-law, as a bricklayer's labourer, before being sent away to Uttoxeter, on a JCB operator's course.

***

I've always treasured the letters that I received over the years for my help at Camp. An interesting one, again from Robin Hazlerigg, arrived after the 1977 Camps. Robin very kindly wrote thank you letters at the end of each Camp (as did Bill Williams) for a number of years.

Dear Alan

I was talking to Skip and he told me what an excellent leader you will make [considering the fact that this year was my eighth as a tent leader, I like to think that Bill meant I would, in the fullness of time, make a decent Skipper]. *You have got the right touch with the boys; you are always loyal* [sadly, I was to throw that assessment in Bill's face just over a decade later] *and Skipper really appreciates your help very much indeed. I think he believes you "belong" to the Camp by this time, and as usual, he hopes to see you again next year.*

Will you give my good wishes to your sister Carmel, who was always so helpful at the Girl's Camp [which unfortunately was very short-lived] *at Condover. I hope she is well and happy.*

Yours sincerely

Mrs G M Hazlerigg.

Bill Williams had the idea of starting a Holiday Camp for "under-privileged" boys because it seemed obvious from where he was standing that girls living in similar circumstances were being welcomed into family homes in the countryside for a holiday but no-one wanted boys; or not "that sort" (my sort) of boy. And as referred to by Mrs Hazlerigg above, a girls' camp was started some ten years or so after Bill's first Camp proper. The irony is, their camp didn't stand the test of time, for various reasons; one being the unsatisfactory behaviour of the young ladies - bless them!

The letters written by the lads, the staff, and just the occasional visitor to our great Camp were almost always written to convey one thing – their thanks. And it was always nice for Bill (and later me) to receive them. Bill's postal deliveries were regular throughout the year, from one Camp to the next; such was the love and respect he commanded.

The following letter to Bill, from the one and only Sid Cliffe, I feel encompasses everything I say above about letter writing – and receiving:

Dear Sir

Thank you for your letter, I love getting letters from you especially. But as you can see by the above address (HMP The Dana, Shrewsbury) things have changed for me since our last meeting. I'm sorry Skip.

I would have liked to have come on Summer Camp again. I really enjoyed the last one. I've never had so much fun in my whole life. I loved working with the children and since last Camp, some of them have written to me. I've replied to every one of them, and said thank you for the photographs they sent me.

I will always remember all the great songs we sang, especially your daughter Debbie's favourite; 'There's a Worm at the Bottom of the Garden'. Brilliant!

I am sorry for letting you down Mr Williams, but I will be

*available to help next year if you want me. I hope you write
back Sir.*
Yours sincerely
Mr S Cliffe.

This lovely man first came to help us in 1975. The above was
written a few months afterwards. He got himself into a bit of
bother; nothing outrageous, for which he paid a hefty price. Sid
Cliffe (who only managed two Camps in all) remains one of the
"all-time favourites". Whoever you were on Camp and whatever
role you occupied, you couldn't fail to become a fan of "Silly
Sid". Our late friend was game for anything and everything.
Whichever group of lads Sid was asked to look after quickly grew
to love him and his antics. God bless him.

Following the 1978 Camps, Bill received this letter from a lad
who lived at the time, in Walsall. It's a pretty shocking letter
but has a nice twist at the end:

Dear Skipper
*Sorry for not writing as I have been in hospital with two
damaged legs, one broken arm, a fractured jaw and 11 stitches.
I was going to the shop for my mum and I had a ten-pound note
to get the shopping. When I was going to the shop I dropped the
ten-pound note and I saw it blowing away so I ran after it and
picked it up. Just then a car came skidding off the road to avoid*

an old lady and it crashed into me.

I couldn't remember a thing after that. I was knocked out for two days. I was in something called a coma. My mum said it was on the news, but the first thing I said when I woke up was what happened to the money. She said I lost it, but it doesn't matter. She told me not to worry about it. So the first thing I am going to do when I am well is get a little job so as I can pay back the money, do you think that would be right Skipper?

Well must go now [here's the twist] *but do not mention anything about my accident in your next letter or my mum will think I am telling my business to people.*
Goodbye for now
Yours
NGH
p.s. write as soon as you can.

I have nothing to say on whether the accident actually occurred or not; the car mounting the pavement to avoid an old lady who must have been in the road. And I certainly have no reason to doubt the lad's words. It was just an amusing end to such a serious letter.

Bill, like us all, had no idea that the Camps of 1978 would be his last on farmer Jack Williams' very ideal field. He was destined to be dealt a most cruel hand by fate, which would rule him out of any part (save a fleeting visit, which in itself was an achievement) of both Camps in 1979. It proved to be the last year ever on that wonderful piece of "heaven". Our days on Jack's land were numbered!

An important letter of notice was sent to the local press by Bill in early June of 1978. It was an invitation to come along to an 'open day' in an effort to raise much-needed funds:

Dear Sir/Madam

The Longmynd Adventure Camps this year will be held at Minton, Church Stretton, Shropshire, from 28th July to 7th August; and from 11th August to 21st August. I enclose a leaflet explaining the aims and object of the Camp and would like to invite you to a Press 'Open Afternoon' from 2pm on Thursday 1st August whilst one of our Camps is in progress.

This is our first major appeal to the public, and your support would encourage us, and hopefully be to our mutual benefit. We shall obviously try to preserve the anonymity of the children attending, but I am sure you will find the Camp newsworthy and also a lot of human interest.

The boys this year will be aged nine to thirteen and will be from the Wolverhampton; Dudley; Walsall and Birmingham areas, and also from here in Shropshire.

The Camp will be signposted from the A49 at Marshbrook, between Craven Arms and Church Stretton.

It would help enormously if you could please complete the

attached slip, and return it in the envelope provided. Thank you.

Yours faithfully

W F Williams, Chairman

Bill wrote to me on 9th June 1978. He had apparently been trying to contact me for some time. Why that should have been difficult for him I don't know as my memory is void of any logical reason for this. Happily, however, all was well as he replied to my latest correspondence. Bill's letter I feel shows that he now considered me an important member of his field staff. This year, though, proved to be my last in this position; well, for eighteen years, anyway!

Dear Alan

Thanks for your letter. I was beginning to wonder what had happened, and had imagined all sorts of things! I even wrote to your mother's address but got no reply. Anyway, so glad to hear that everything is ok; and even more pleased to know that you can come to Camp again. I think we shall finish up with more boys than ever this year... and probably less staff! Lots of development since last we met. Hopefully we shall have our own permanent site from 1979 onwards; all we need is £6,000! I look forward to seeing you soon, regards to Tina.

Best wishes

Bill

The 1978 Camps rolled around and the people who turned up to help got stuck into their appointed task of helping to provide another most memorable holiday for (as the press phrased it) "socially deprived boys". The local press showing up during either the first or second Camp was by this time almost a given. And, generally speaking, it was good that they came along because as Bill very often said, "all publicity is good for us".

One of the photographs published in the *Shropshire Star* during the1978 Camps contained an error regarding my service to the Camp. The picture showed me holding a football, with the caption:

The Longmynd Adventure Camp is in full swing again this year at Minton, Church Stretton, providing holidays for socially deprived children from Wolverhampton, Dudley, Walsall, Birmingham and Shropshire. Alan Scriven (25) first came to the camp as a boy in 1964 [it was in fact 1965] *but for the past nine years he has taken part of his annual holiday helping others, in this instance, a little football coaching for the lads.*

Another mistake in the report was that in fact all of my annual leave was taken up by helping at Camp, not part of it.

Unlike the majority of Bill's staff, I had experienced no problems (as yet) with booking the time off work to assist at both Camps. My bosses were very accommodating when I explained to them (on joining the company) that I needed "special dispensation" regarding my annual summer holidays.

It was an entirely different 'kettle of fish' a few years later, however, when in 1981 I tried my hand at selling double-glazing for Everest. Although it was a self-employed position (they only paid a 17.5% commission on any orders one managed to close) my regional manager refused point-blank to sanction my request for cover on my 'patch' whilst I was away at Camp. I tried in vain to explain that my absence could be looked upon as a "working holiday" (well Camp **was** work, and bloody hard work at that!). But nothing moved him or swayed his resolve. The problem he had, however, was a total failure to appreciate **my** resolve!

After trying my level best to arrive at an amicable solution, all he said was, 'I've made my position clear. I can't allow you to take a holiday for whatever good cause it might be, at this moment in time. Therefore, I have to tell you that if you disobey my decision, your position with this company will not be resumed when your good deed is done.'

I didn't even consider his threat. Yes, I had a five-year-old son to think about; Tina was working, though, part-time, at the Staffordshire Volunteer pub near where we lived. So I reckoned we probably wouldn't starve to death if I was forced to look for alternative employment upon returning, with Marc, from Camp. My wife was very supportive and I've always been grateful to her for that. Not once at any time during our thirteen-year marriage did she put even the slightest pressure on me to forego

Camp... if you disregard the second Camp of 1979, when I ended up bringing three-year-old Marc with me rather than missing it!

Upon returning from the 1981 Camps I did attempt to contact my regional boss at Everest but it was a fruitless effort. He refused to take my calls so I understood and accepted his "unspoken message". I was out of work until almost four months after the birth of our second son, Tom, in July 1982.

The circumstances which led to my elevation to "high office" at Camp in 1979 are well documented in my first book.

One of my tent leaders that notable Year of the Child was the very likeable, and indeed extremely able, Malcolm Webster. Mal (or "Webby" as he was sometimes addressed) was a local Church Stretton lad with whom I had thoroughly enjoyed working on Camp the previous year. We became good friends and I trusted him implicitly. Malcolm was a great tent leader from 1978 until 1986, covering some thirteen Camps. I thought it would be a good thing if Malcolm told the story himself, of how he came to be at the Longmynd Adventure Camp, so here are his own words, written during the summer of 2017:

My involvement with the LAC came quite out of the blue (having previously never known or heard anything about it). In the summer of 1978 I was celebrating being eighteen, and now able to access pubs legally! It was at one of these pub gatherings in July, at the Kings Arms in Church Stretton with some Venture Scout friends of mine, when a certain Mr Bill Williams walked in and ordered a pint at the bar. Bill noticed Dave Spurling (whose father had been a helper on Bill's Camp for some time) and came over for a chat. Bill seemed to me a very confident and pleasant sort of chap. He mentioned that he was looking to recruit voluntary helpers for his Camp. The end result was that a meeting would be convened in one week, to discuss the Camp in more detail.

After a short discussion Bill asked if any of us were interested in helping at the forthcoming Camp in a fortnight's time. I made the commitment there and then, saying 'yes, I'll give it a go'.

I spent the next two weeks wondering if I had made the right decision. Simon Lumley (my friend and fellow Venture Scout) and I met several times to discuss our decision to help Bill. Deciding to commit ourselves to this unknown challenge, however, we both visited the Camp on the Thursday afternoon, prior to the boys' arrival the following day. As we approached the Camp, the initial nerves kicked in as we hoped for a friendly welcome.

Unfortunately, the "friendly welcome" didn't quite happen as we were suspiciously (it seemed) eyed up by several of the helpers already there. To our relief, however, Bill appeared with a very friendly face and welcomed us both to Camp. As we walked around the field we were introduced to a couple of helpers, both of whom spoke a strange version of English; the sort I associated with hardened Wolves fans (it turned out they both supported Manchester United). Neither of these two blokes came across as friendly, in fact, they both appeared somewhat uneasy with our presence. Simon and I put this down to the fact that we were locals, and therefore didn't fit into this imported piece of the West Midlands, on the Long Mynd. Their handshakes, however, were a little more 'encouraging' and we took this as a good sign.

We drove away to spend the night at our homes, and during the evening we sat down with Simon's parents and discussed whether we ought to drop out or not. But after another cup of tea and a nice slice of cake I said it was too late to drop out, and the Wolverhampton guys were probably friendlier than they initially appeared. With the decision made, we set off for Camp on the following morning to prepare for the boys' arrival at approximately 2pm; thus beginning my nine-year association with The Longmynd Adventure Camp, during which time I helped on thirteen Holiday Camps.

At this point it is worth mentioning that the two guys from Wolverhampton were Alan Scriven and Tony Hammond. So much for first impressions!

The first Camp of 1978 began in earnest, and I really took to it. The boys were a great bunch who clearly appreciated the fact that we were doing something for them on a purely voluntary basis. They didn't ask for much (unlike many of today's youngsters); they were happy with the simple activities *which they felt a part of. What most of them were looking for, I thought, was someone to simply take an interest in them, enabling them to have a 'role model' whom they could look up to and respect. I was generally impressed with their resilience, and friendly nature; especially when one considers what some of them had already been through in their short lives.*

Discipline was maintained by way of a Tent Competition (see below), which I took very seriously, and set out to win it right from the off! On day three we got our noses in front for the first time; feeling very proud to be presented with the Camp Staffs. It was a privilege for the tent group leading the contest, to be presented with the wooden staffs (sticks), and much was made of the presentation by the Skipper as he handed one to each boy (and leader depending on numbers) telling a far-fetched tale of the history of each staff he handed over. Unfortunately we lost the staffs on the following day; regaining them on day five, after which we never looked back, and I won the competition with my lads from Tent Six on my very first Camp. This was despite discovering that the tent competition was rigged from the start, through to the final couple of days. The final two days gave the Skipper a little peace of mind that the best group had actually won. The competition was rigged, Skipper explained at the end of Camp, because it was his only way (indirectly) of keeping discipline during the ten days, i.e. points merit and demerit to keep every tent in close competition.

Bill also explained that this method was also a way of stopping Alan Scriven and his Tent One from winning every year!

I quickly learnt that Alan was always the man to beat. Bill rightly wanted us all to run our tents as Alan did; even so, victory for Tent One didn't occur too often. His attempts to win were regularly thwarted by the Skipper making some 'creative' decisions when distributing precious tent points.

My favourite activity was always the 'Ghost Hunt', but another great memory of 1978 was all the singing. Alan certainly had a lost vocation here. Alan's regular and excellent renditions of Roger Whittaker's hit 'The Last Farewell' (among others) have kept this fantastic song firmly stuck in my mind ever since! And to this day, every time I hear it fond memories of the LAC come flooding back. Alan, Owen Lewis (from Church Stretton) and I later formed a singing group called "The Minton Moguls", after a suggestion by Bill to encourage the lads to go to the brook every morning for a wash. We were a huge success.

My hunch that the Wolverhampton guys would be fine proved correct. The staff members were great fun, and I've never laughed as much over ten days as I did on Camp. Alan and Tony became good friends of mine for the whole of my time with the LAC; and Alan, for quite some time afterwards.

I left Camp that year feeling I had achieved something really positive. As a person from a more middle class background from the boys... and the majority of the staff, I felt I had given something back to those who were not as fortunate as I had been.

Bill Williams rang me during the Spring of 1979, enquiring of my availability to help on Camp again. I said "count me in."

How shocked I was then to receive a call from Alan just before the start of Camp 1979. He told me that Bill had suffered a very serious heart attack, and would therefore be unable to take charge of this year's Camp. He said that he had been asked to Skipper the Camp; adding that he would be very pleased to have me on board. Alan promoted me to Tent Two; and Tony Hammond became the new leader of the prestigious Tent One. I felt that out of nowhere I had been promoted to third in command, which was quite uplifting at the time.

Alan's style of leadership was very different to Bill's. He was a lot younger, and related well to the boys (having himself been on Camp as a boy). There was no shortage of "mickey taking" as Alan was able to expand his humour through his more 'overseeing' role as Skipper, and he also rose to another level with his singing "career" as he increased his song repertoire. I remember 'Tell Laura I Love Her' being a massive success that year.

Happily, Bill recovered from illness to take charge in 1980 of the very first Camps on the LAC's new and permanent premises just up the lane. Alan was permanently installed as Bill's official number two, taking the title of 'Bosun' the following year.

Although memories of the 1980 Camps are somewhat sketchy, I know that the first one gave me the most pleasure. I had a fantastic bunch of lads; all terrific to work with, and we won the tent competition... despite the efforts of our Bosun to hijack our campaign!

The toilets were very basic at this early stage of the new site's development, and the boys nicknamed it "the kack shack".

As the years rolled on I settled into my role as a tent leader, and by and large I really enjoyed my time with the Camp. Although I didn't realise it at the time however, the Camps of 1986 were to be my last ever! I had by now become a teacher and my career in this profession was accelerating at a pace, and it became evident that I needed a break from working with children during the summer holidays. I had also purchased my first house, so the holidays were needed for the obligatory DIY.

I met with Bill during the spring of 1987 and told him of my decision to quit. It was time, I told him, for me to move on with my life and new challenges. Bill was very sad to lose me, but fully accepted my reasons for calling time on my illustrious Camp career. Sadly, after that meeting, I never saw Bill Williams again.

A couple of years after my last Camp, I was in my classroom at the school in Telford that I worked at, when a member of my class approached me and said: "Mr Webster do you know Alan the bus driver?" From this I discovered that Alan Scriven had moved to Telford and was working for the Midland Red Bus

Company; and one of his routes ran right past my school. This led to us meeting up again, and I visited him at his Dawley home on several occasions. Eventually though, Alan moved back to Wolverhampton, and we lost touch again for a while.

Happily though, we have now regained contact, and speak regularly via social media mainly.
Malcolm Webster
Tent/Cabin Leader 1978 - 1986

Sadly, Mal passed away on 14th May 2018 after a courageous battle with cancer. God bless you, mate, and thank you.

I mentioned in my first book how highly I rated Malcolm Webster as a leader, and indeed a friend. I didn't realise, however, until reading his memoirs, that Tony and I appeared unfriendly initially. It wasn't intentional; we took to the youngster like a duck to water. I thought the world of Malcolm and he was without doubt my first choice Bosun. If only he'd agreed to my invitation in 1990, and returned to the fold. Malcolm's exceptional teaching career, however, proves that he made the right decision to leave us. What a tragic pity that his career was so cruelly cut short.

My late friend Alan Preece was another of my helpers in 1979. Alan, a fellow former beneficiary, knew the workings of Camp like the back of his hand, and it was down to people such as him and Malcolm Webster that I made such a great success of standing in for Bill that year. Also deserving of a mention for his outstanding contribution in 1979 is my brother David. He, like Tony and Malcolm, gave many years of dedicated service to the Camp. David was a good 'utility man' in that he could turn his hand to whatever job he was asked to do, be it in the kitchen or in the field. He wasn't bad at a bit of poetry-writing (usually for the Campfire evening), either.

The only other person (in my opinion) who could perform likewise was Dean Nightingale, who initially arrived in 1983 as one of the boys.

***

In 1979 I was in my third year at Jenks and Cattell. By this time I had taken up the position, when required, of JCB Operator. The company sent me on a two-week course at the Bamford's base in Uttoxeter and I really enjoyed it. My colleagues on the building maintenance team at Jenks's were Ivor Bateman and Arthur Whittingham (bricklayers) as well as Colin Burford and Ronnie Newall (carpenters). We had a painter called Phil Denton who I knew well from school. Martin Walters, Patrick Harte (my then father-in-law) and I were the labourers, and we were under the charge of Don Smith, the foreman carpenter. I enjoyed my time at this place, until I was made redundant in 1980.

Following my redundancy, I just "bummed around" for a

while. I couldn't get any full-time work no matter how hard I tried. In the end I was forced to sign on the dole. I hated this degrading 'ritual' of once a fortnight having to go to the Unemployment Benefits Office in Temple Street, Wolverhampton. This spell, short as it was, of having no work prompted me to write the following poem:

An Untouchable Brand!

You've finished on Friday, the gaffer said.

And the thought of redundancy went straight to my head; no more getting up early, late mornings instead, when all that I'll do is lie in my bed!

Nothing to do and all day to 'perform'; running around like a leaf in a storm. Lost and dejected, society's cruel. Just watch me bounce back though, I'm nobody's fool.

But that's some time ago, and I've still got no job; no money in my pocket........ not even a bob!

My clothes are decaying and there's nothing I can do. I can't afford a haircut, and I've a hole in my shoe.

The jobcentre's useless; a complete waste of money. Two hundred bees fighting for just one drop of honey.

The dole is as bad, they don't understand.

To them, we are AN UNTOUCHABLE BRAND!

I couldn't bear hanging around the house, getting under Tina's feet at every turn! So I kept out of her way as much as I could by walking everywhere (looking for work, mostly) and keeping our large garden in fine fettle. Our home in Somerford Gardens, Bushbury, was a corner house so we had a massive rear garden which was bordered by our neighbours and Collingwood School.

It was this situation which led to me trying my hand with Everest, selling double glazing door-to-door. I made a steady living for myself and my family but wasn't with the company long enough to even begin attempting to carve out a career in that business. So, after having my time with "the best" abruptly cut short I turned, for a very short time, to selling small security items door-to-door for some right dodgy geezer whose name escapes my memory! I never would have thought that in a few years' time I would be doing exactly the same (for a short time) for a certain Mr Bill Williams BEM.

Winds of Change

In 1982 I successfully applied for a manager's position at a recently opened "seconds" tile warehouse, which also had a Crown Paints franchise. The business was called Tameside Trade Paints Ltd. Crown Paints were, at that time, sponsors of Liverpool Football Club; and after about a year of the company being in business in Wolverhampton, the company arranged a promotional evening at the premises in Lower Stafford Street. Two of the football club's biggest 'stars' were asked to attend the function so I, as manager, had to have my photo taken with Alan Hansen and Craig Johnston... with the trophies Liverpool were holding at the time: the League Division One Championship, the Charity Shield, and the 'Milk' (League) Cup.

I hated that job, my so-called colleagues, and everyone connected with the ownership of the damn place, except for a lovely bloke called Norman Fielding. Norman was a good man, fair and true.

In the autumn of 1985 I was suspected of a terrible act of theft whilst employed at this place! I was absolutely innocent, though, and if the person/people who actually committed the crime just happen to be reading this book; hold your disgraceful heads in shame!! The guilty party knows who they are; they have to know because they are guilty of a crime that they tried their level best to fit me up with. It's a terrible feeling when you are accused of something like I was, and you know that the rat(s) are in the same room as you, breathing the same air, and lying through their rotten teeth!

Due to the fact that the directors refused, despite my regular requests, to install a safe, I had to hide the day's takings (and the following day's "float") on the premises. The following morning, the cash would be retrieved and our young labourer was sent to the bank to pay in the takings from the previous day. At the close of business on the day before the theft, I told the other person who was now working in the same role as me that I was putting the money in an empty Solvite bucket. The bucket was placed at the very bottom of a stack of others before we all went home. When I went to get the previous day's takings from the hiding place the next day, the money was missing.

I didn't pay much heed to this initially because I thought my colleague must have already sent the lad to the bank. I made my way down to the cellar where they were both working, to confirm this. To my horror and disbelief my colleague told me he had been "nowhere near the money" and neither, apparently, had our young labourer.

To cut a long story short I telephoned Mr Hoffman, one of our directors (who was also a solicitor), and explained the situation. His reply was, "Ring the police and when they arrive get them to phone me." This I did and when the police arrived one officer spoke to our director on the telephone. Upon replacing the receiver he promptly arrested me on suspicion of theft! To say I was gobsmacked is an understatement. My colleague said absolutely nothing as I was led away to the waiting police car. At the station I was put into a cell for what seemed like an age, before being taken to an interview room where I was interrogated before being released on police bail. Between that day and the day before I was to surrender my bail not one of my bosses spoke to me, despite my several attempts to contact them. My "colleagues" also kept their distance as much as they possibly could. And I continued doing my job as I had prior to all this shit! Why wouldn't I!

On the evening before I was due to return to the police station I had a call from the police to say I did not need to keep the appointment and that the matter was now closed. Just a short while after this, however, I was, without warning, made redundant; even though I was the senior manager, and had been from day one of my employment. My colleague with whom I had hitherto shared the managerial responsibilities was unceremoniously (and mysteriously) dismissed!

Redundancy is another form of dismissal, which can be appealed against. But there was no point in my case. I had been fitted up like a kipper! I remain to this day willing to undergo a lie detector test at any time. **I did not steal that money**!! It is worth mentioning, I feel, that at the time and for many years prior to and after this matter, I was regularly in the company of His Honour Judge Peter Northcote; former police superintendent Pat Hazlehurst, and former police sergeant Bill Williams. To have stolen that money (and robbed the hand that fed me) would not have stood me in good stead with them.

***

During the first Camp of 1979, when I skippered the Camp in Bill's absence due to illness, Roy "Butcher" Williams asked me if I would be willing to try and get some 'recognition' for Bill's extraordinary charity work over the lifetime of the Camp, and earlier. Roy said that he had already done as much as he thought he could, and asked if I would therefore be interested in "having a go". I told him then that I didn't see how someone like me could possibly succeed where he hadn't been able to and so declined his suggestion.

Despite trying, though, I couldn't get the fact out of my head that Bill had thus far received no formal recognition by way of the Honours system for his unstinting commitment to the Longmynd Adventure Camp and the other worthy causes which are mentioned in detail in my first book. In 1982 I decided to tell Roy that I would, if he still thought it worthwhile, do what I could. On 14th April 1982 Roy wrote back to me:

Dear Alan

It was a very pleasant surprise to receive your letter.

I made attempts to get an honour for Bill on three separate occasions; 1975, 1977 and 1979. I am enclosing as much of the correspondence as I can find to give you some idea of the scope of these efforts. I had a reply from Buckingham Palace, but seem to have left it at home, and I am now at the office.

The minister who could recommend an honour for an enterprise such as the Boys' Camp is the Secretary for Education and Science; currently Sir Keith Joseph. I have previously been in touch with two of his predecessors, Shirley Williams and Mark Carlisle, without success, and have also approached them via MPs who are personal friends; and also the MPs for several divisions of Shropshire. I am convinced that somewhere along the line of Bill's past police service, some "incident", probably very minor, took place which has had the effect of blocking him from the Honours system.

Mrs (Pat) Hazlehurst, herself a former police superintendent (Shropshire's very first female superintendent) inclines to this opinion. So, Alan, I do not feel I can do anything more than I have.

On the other hand, if you feel inclined to have a go, as a graduate of the Camp, I will help in any way I can.
All the very best
Roy.

With regard to Roy's comments about the possibility of something happening during Bill's 25-year police career, which could have blocked any award, we have to consider the fact that

Bill was, in his time as a constable, chair of the Police Federation, representing all ranks below Superintendent. It is quite within reason to assume that Bill could have 'upset' one, or any number, of his senior officers whilst vigorously going about the duties and responsibilities of his position.

Bill was eventually recognised for his immeasurable charity work, in the form of the British Empire Medal, in 1983, which happened to be the Camp's silver jubilee year! Naturally I, like many others, was extremely pleased that he had at last found some favour with the "powers that be" but it should have been much more. People have been knighted for less!

When one considers the excessive awards lavishly offered to the likes of so-called pop stars, film stars and footballers, for example, it really brings home the fact that Bill was not given the award he truly deserved. Call it bias if you wish, but I sincerely believe the man should have been knighted.

When I went to Buckingham Palace to receive the MBE from the Queen in 2001, I was in the same room as a head teacher from Telford, who was there to be invested with a knighthood. Surely Bill Williams was as much entitled to this honour as our gentleman friend from Telford? I'm not bemoaning the award; I simply feel, strongly, that Bill was, in the very least, equally as deserving.

The following is a letter written by me, published in the *Shropshire Star*, after Bill's award was made public:

Sir, I would like to comment on the deserved recognition shown to one of Shropshire's most well-known sons, for his abundance of voluntary charity work over the last twenty-five years.

I refer to Mr Bill Williams of Montford Bridge, Shrewsbury; chair, and founder of the Longmynd Adventure Camp – a registered charity providing country holidays at a beautiful spot near Church Stretton, for socially deprived children of the West Midlands – who was awarded the BEM in the New Year's Honours.

And how fitting that his efforts should be recognised by this honour, in the silver jubilee year of perhaps his finest personal achievement; building a permanent organisation to bring welcome relief, albeit short and sweet, from the humdrum of everyday life, to the many hundreds of children (myself included) over the past quarter century.

I first met Bill in 1965, as a beneficiary of his kindness. And annual experience of working on Camp with him has shown me what a dedicated and resolute man he is. His hard work, however, inevitably brought its consequences, culminating in a heart attack in 1979, from which happily he recovered and returned to the helm the following year.

So to the good folk of Shropshire, hats off please in salute to your friend and mine; a real Shropshire lad, famed only for his unselfishness and a burning desire to help others.

Alan Scriven Beneficiary; Camp Staff Member; Committee Member of the LAC.

A short time after publication of the above, I received a wonderful letter from a friend of Pat Hazlehurst. I only wish the good lady's appreciation of the Camp and her hopes for its future could have borne the fruit she dreamed of:

Dear Alan
Having seen your superb letter in the 'Star' I have to write and congratulate you on such a super letter.

Your letter really was an excellent way to express not only your thanks, but those of many others too, who perhaps could not put it into words; you did, and I am sure Bill – even Bill - will have glowed with pride.

Yes it is a super venture, and long may it continue; and with people like you involved it will last forever!

Well done Alan. Keep up the good work.
Miss V A Wilson
Alma Street
Shrewsbury.

Our new and permanent base, just up the lane from Jack Williams's field was seen as a 'godsend' by one and all, when we were finally able to hold our first Camp there in 1980. By 1982, however, we still hadn't got mains electricity installed. In an effort to try and help us raise the required funds, the *Shropshire Star* and the *Express and Star* kindly published an article headed:

Camp needs £2,500 to switch on

Below are a few excerpts from the article:

A Shropshire adventure camp which has provided hundreds of youngsters with the rare chance of a holiday is in urgent need of £2,500 to provide an electric supply...

The camp – now in its 24th year – will be giving 100 boys a holiday in two ten-day sessions, starting on July 29.

"Obviously we would like the electric to be in by then because we need it for lighting; and preparing food," said retired policeman Bill Williams of 10 Shrawardine, near Shrewsbury. "We now have this permanent building, which has a kitchen, staffroom, games/dining area, and toilets on our own field. Church Stretton Round Table has paid to have it wired for us," he said.

One of the members of staff now helping Bill is Alan Scriven of Wolverhampton, who at the age of 12 first began his association with the camp in 1965. Alan is now the official 'number two' at the camp.

"I have been every year since 1965," Alan said, "and I love it, just like so many others."

Eventually, the Home Office agreed to foot the bill for the installation of mains electricity.

Fundraising continued as ever! The WRVS eased the pressure of financing the holidays when in 1982 it agreed to increase its contribution to £20 per child. And amongst other kind sponsors of my 'Longmynd Hike' efforts, Judge Peter Northcote sent me a cheque for £30. In his accompanying letter he explained that £10 was from himself, £10 from John Huxley, and £10 from Mr Goodman of the Wroxeter Hotel. Every little helped.

***

I was happy and contented with my life in the early eighties; the awful incident during my time at the Crown Paints franchise, as mentioned above, being the only negative. We now had our second son, Thomas, and everything was rosy.

My friendship with Bill Williams was in tip-top condition; we were spending regular weekends together walking, mainly on the Long Mynd, or meeting up at the local hostelries of Shrewsbury and Church Stretton. I loved being in Bill's company; he was a font of knowledge and I was a good listener. Terry Pugh often joined us but didn't really take part in any of our deep and interesting conversations; he was happy just to tag along and enjoy the walk, or the pub. Bill had been retired from the police force for over a decade by this time but old habits die hard, as they say, and many of our chats focused around law and order, which Bill was still very much interested in. I remember us having very different views about the coal miners' strike in 1984, producing some intense vocals between the two of us because as well as being a former police officer, Bill was also a strong supporter of our (then) lady prime minister! He would take me (and John Preece sometimes) to the Conservative club in Shrewsbury and he always made a point of acknowledging Maggie's large framed photograph, which hung in the main room. Bill was also a member of the Shrewsbury Police Choir and he tried his level best to get me to join too... no thanks, Skipper!

As mentioned in my first book, the main event of 1983 (outside of the actual Camps, and Bill's BEM award) was the charity football match I helped to organise, along with fellow committee member (and grand-daughter of Clement Atlee) Joanna Pinniger (as she was then). The match took place at Shrewsbury in the autumn and featured the *Minder* star Dennis Waterman's "Celebrity XI", playing a team of Wolverhampton Wanderers former first-team players, led by the one and only Derek Dougan.

On 5th November, the following was published in the *Express and Star*:

Wolves made our Day

Following the recent criticism of Derek Dougan and the Wolves, I feel I must write and lend a little bit of genuine support for Mr Dougan, and company.

On Sunday 16th October our charity held a football match at Shrewsbury, to mark our twenty-fifth anniversary. Derek Dougan was invited to come along and participate; with the actor Dennis Waterman and members of his celebrity soccer team.

Not only did Mr Dougan accept; he also brought along all the necessary wherewithal to play the game, e.g. football strips, boots, and balls etc. As well, he persuaded a good number of well-known former players to give their services free, including Graham Hawkins, Jim Barron, Willie Carr, Ernie Hunt, Eddie Clamp, Terry Wharton, Bobby Thompson, Freddie Kemp, Barry Stobart and Gerry Harris. He even brought along the Wolves physio, George Denjend.

It was a great day for everyone involved, and the spectators. We managed to raise £600, and I will always be grateful to Derek Dougan and Wolverhampton Wanderers FC for their kindness; enthusiasm, and willingness to please.

Alan Scriven, Longmynd Adventure Camp committee member.

As per usual, fundraising was paramount with Bill and to this end he produced (in 1984) a leaflet, which was circulated far and wide, in the hope of bringing in more cash to boost our meagre coffers.

The four-page leaflet, A5 in size, was very well designed. At the top of the front page it read:

The Longmynd Adventure Camp Appeal
Will you please help us to raise money?

Below that heading was a boxed letter from one of the lads:

Dear Skipper
I hope you are feeling well. Thank you for the beautiful holiday
that you gave me and for the songs that you learned me and
thank you for the lemonade and the book prize. Thank you for
the trip to Shrewsbury I enjoyed it very much. Thank you for
supplying the equipment for the sports; and the raincoat.
Bye for now
See you next year
From Clive Pearce
Tent 1 'Champs'

Page two was headed:

THE LONGMYND ADVENTURE CAMP

Then followed a detailed explanation of what the Camp was
about; its aims; a short history of its being, and of course a plea
for much-needed donations. Below are a few excerpts from the
leaflet:

The people of South Shropshire and particularly those who live in the shadow of the Long Mynd will know of the work done by the Adventure Camp. The object of this pamphlet is to bring those who know about our efforts up to date and, we hope, stir the interest of those who have not yet come to know of our work.

The Camp is a registered charity, established to provide country holidays for boys between nine and fourteen years. The boys come from deprived backgrounds and have had little or no opportunity to enjoy a holiday. Many of the boys have never been away from home, and few have ever camped.

Most of the holiday is spent outdoors in the beautiful Shropshire hills. A Sports Day; lots of swimming, and a trip to the seaside are included in the busy programme.

In 1978 the committee launched an appeal to raise £6,000. This money was needed to purchase a permanent site for the Camp, and to build Dining and Recreational facilities. The target was achieved, with the majority of the money coming from three sponsors: The Intermediate Fund; The Llankelly Trust, and Shropshire's own Walker Trust. Additionally, many firms and private individuals in the West Midlands area gave us generous help and support.

The permanent site was purchased in 1978, and we held our first Camps on it in 1980, after much work to prepare the site to a somewhat acceptable state...

Since 1981 considerable progress has been made with the facilities at the Camp site.

The Camps held in 1984 provided holidays for 100 boys; 20 of whom were Shropshire lads, with the remainder hailing from Wolverhampton, Sandwell and Walsall, etc. I really believe it was an unforgettable experience for the boys, and this was evident from the tears of some of them as the coach pulled away, taking the lads home.

And again, we gave a large number of these boys their very first view of the sea; which was exciting for us too.

This year, the contribution of the recommending body, towards the cost of each child, was £2 per day; the balance kindly provided by the generosity of, mostly the people of Shropshire...

No contribution is too small (or too large), and the benefits which accrue to the children who enjoy these holidays are so great we must not neglect them.

Thank you

The back page listed the committee members of the day. Sadly, none are involved with today's Longmynd Adventure Camp.

The middle of the decade was a period of time when we worked hard to secure a mains water supply. We duly succeeded, as always due largely to the few committed people who had our best interests at heart.

As well as this important project going on, I was planning a walk from the WRVS offices in Wolverhampton to the gate of the Longmynd Adventure Camp. First and foremost to raise cash for the water fund but also as a way of celebrating my twenty-five-year association with the Camp. I was dreading the walk if I'm honest but it turned out to be one of the easiest things I've ever done. And it was a great day, too. Bill drove the back-up vehicle and kept us all entertained with his clever use of the PA system on board.

Another successful fundraiser in May of the same year (1986) was a two-day event at the Shropshire and West Midlands Agricultural Society showground in Shrewsbury. John Preece and I ran a tombola of sorts during the West Midlands Show, raising a bit more towards the water fund. We put the idea to Bill in early February and he duly contacted the Society's committee regarding requirements for setting up a stall.

Mr A J Hall replied to Bill on 18th February:

I thank you for your letter of 5th Feb 1986 asking for details of a possible site at this year's show.

Normally, our minimum site outside is 20ft frontage x 30ft depth, costing £80.00 plus vat, and two years' membership and entry fee at the special charity rates. As a concession to charities we would be prepared to let you have a 10ft frontage plot for £40.00 plus one year's membership, plus entry fee and vat. The plot would be near the wildlife area at the South East corner of the Showground.

Wishing you all the best with your work for the young.

Earlier in the year, on 21st February, I wrote to Sergeant Kendall of Wolverhampton police, asking what the chances were of him organising, or helping me to organise, a charity football match between Wolves Police and members of the Shropshire Constabulary, based in Shrewsbury. My contact in Shrewsbury was constable Andy Preston. Sadly, there was no favourable outcome from this latest attempt at adding to our coffers.

The reason behind my approach to the police was down to the fact that Bill was a former policeman in Shropshire (and over the years the Camp had benefitted from the West Mercia Constabulary helping us in whatever capacity it could), plus the fact that the lads by now hailed, for the most part, from Wolverhampton and Shropshire

Ironically, it was the water problem that made most of the reading in my report to the committee, on the 1986 Camps. I began by saying that both Camps had been very successful, and that a new cooker had been fitted during the first Camp. I added that the water had "worked extremely well considering nothing was certain regarding the supply until Camp week."
My report continued:

Once the mains water supply has been installed properly (hopefully in time for the 1987 Camps), we only need to focus on field staff; kitchen staff, and a QM. We cannot any longer afford to have surplus 'staff' on Camp. Furthermore, we must

not allow the Camp to fall into a position whereby it finds itself having to beg more cash from the WRVS than our main sponsors can reasonably afford to give us. Our struggle was emphasised by the fact that this year we had to pay for all the bread we used; a total in excess of two hundred pounds.

The committee, by and large, accepted Bill's and my decisions on the actual running of the Camps but even if it didn't we usually went ahead anyway; always believing that it was our right to do so, bearing in mind the original reason that the committee was formed back in the seventies.

The final years of the eighties decade weren't the happiest of my life. In March 1987 my mother died. Her passing affected me greatly. I loved her with all my heart.

A short time after she left us I wrote a tribute to her:

My Mother

She was the morning sunshine of each new day
The fresh rain that falls from the sky.
She was the golden daffodil of early Spring;
Why did she have to die?
She was the love that kept us all together,
A shoulder when we needed to cry.
We took it for granted she'd always be there
Why did she have to die?
She was the dainty lily on the shimmering pond,

Winds of Change

The robin that flew in the air;
The peeling bell of the country church,
The fun of the English fair.
She was each smooth pebble on the river-bed,
Each twinkling star of the night;
She was the mighty ocean, a grain of sand,
The brightest shining light.
She was the soft white snow of winter,
The fledgling just flown from the nest.
She was the ripened fruit of the orchard;
The purest and the best.
When I consider all that my mother meant,
I can't help wanting to cry.
She was the rock solid patron of all that is good;
Why did she have to die?

PC Bill Williams – an early picture.

Bill and Hetty Williams with daughters Ann and Debbie.

Gerald – the first boy to holiday at the Williams' household – and the tormentor of grass snakes!

Mrs Winnie Hull – the first and only WVS lady to help on Camp, from the early 1960s.

With my beloved mum.

With Bill Williams.

With brothers David (left) & Billy (centre).

Me (left) with (l-r) Mick Powell, John Preece and my son Marc.

The infamous Fancy Dress competition (1980s).

Some of the 1997 staff: Steve Phillips, Phil Woods, Tony Hammond, Tom Scriven, Dean Nightingale, Wendy Smith & Neil Harrison (l-r).

Progress through Change

The 1980s ended with a massive shape-shift which shook the whole being of the charity to its core! I don't propose to go over the main reason for this because that sad situation is documented in acute detail in my first book. But the result, following months of negotiations between Bill and the rest of the committee - myself included - was that I was installed as Skipper, after Bill broke all ties with the Camp during the spring of 1990.

Tina and I had been divorced for a couple of years but remained on friendly terms and we both believe this was extremely beneficial to our children. Marc was now somewhat of a veteran camper at the young age of fourteen and I included him in my first staff list. Our youngest lad Tom was about to enjoy only his third Camp because his mother had refused point-blank to let me take him until he was six years old: "He's my babby, you're not taking him to the back of beyond."

The reasons for Marc beginning his Camp career at an earlier age are detailed in my first book.

In a strange way, our break-up and eventual divorce did wonders for our ongoing 'relationship'. Being free from the confines of a full-on partnership allowed us, I feel, to get on with our dual role as parents. And that has stood the test of time brilliantly. A little while after we parted I wrote a short poem about our marriage break-up and was surprised when it was included, at a later date, in a book of poems called *A Blossom of Dreams*:

Lost Love

When the wind blows the trees in the garden we shared, and raindrops fall on the leaf-littered lawn; I remember our togetherness, the day it was born; a love that could not be compared.

At night I sit alone by the fountain of the pond; seemingly protected by the caress of the willow. Whilst passing clouds look down at my wretched state, and try to convince me that you're there, at the gate.

Time is the great healer, or so I am told. But your face I shall see, yet when I am old. And though the bond is now broken and words were not spared; I still yearn for the love that could not be compared.

In truth, there was no "wretched state", broken bonds or harsh words, but it made the poem better, I think.

***

My first year as Skipper (proper) was a rip-roaring success despite my worries and negative feelings during the weeks leading up to it. Much of this success was down to the staff members who in the vast majority had gone the extra mile to ensure that not only did the children have a truly memorable holiday but also that they and I did too. All the time, though, throughout the ten days of the actual Camp, I hoped against hope that Bill would show up. But he didn't; not for six long years! And I know that deep down inside I suffered for this. Bill was my rock! We had enjoyed an almost father-son relationship for twenty-five fantastic years. But the carpet had been savagely pulled from under our friendship by an eternally regrettable decision by yours truly during a farcical committee meeting on an ill-tempered evening in the Skipper's caravan a little time after the 1989 Camps. *The Longmynd Adventure Camp and Me* details the facts and the politics of this, the blackest and bleakest chapter in the whole history of this wonderful place in South Shropshire.

Obviously Bill had his supporters; indeed, I was one of them – which reads, I concede, like a contradiction. Some of these people chose to end their support of the Camp once it was established that Bill's tenure was at an end. I held not one ounce of contempt for their show of support to Bill. I can say right now that had I not been directly involved, I too would have reacted as they did. Francis Rudge and Terry Pugh, both stalwarts of the Camp, never again offered their services. And I never again felt the way I had up to the point when Bill's involvement ended so dramatically!

I had thought that Richard George's help was also consigned to our glorious past after I received a letter from him, dated 12th May 1990. This was a matter of weeks after a fateful committee meeting which resulted in Bill making his future away from the LAC. Richard was a friend of Bill's and so the timing of his letter seemed ominous:

Dear Alan

In response to your request for help, I'm afraid that this year I will be unable to help. This is due to home, work, and personal problems; but has nothing to do with Bill resigning.

Wendy and I have chatted about the situation, which is really awkward to put onto paper.

However, very best wishes and good luck.

Richard George.

I read 'between the lines' as you do, and convinced myself that that was it as far as Richard's assistance was concerned but to my surprise, he offered to help me for part of the 1991 Camp. I gratefully accepted.

I had been elected Skipper after deciding to go for the position because of fear that an 'outsider' would erase all the effort, goodwill and tradition that Bill had worked so hard to build up. And having been granted the opportunity to step into the main role, I intended, with a steely determination, to succeed...

always... in the hope that the true and rightful Skipper would return. When he did, the Camp would hopefully still be in the position it had been at the time he left it: ship-shape.

I did make one or two changes, however – to the programme mainly – but nothing that an occasional visitor might notice, except for the scrapping of the 'Fancy Dress' competition, held religiously during the very busy final afternoon.

My staff for the 1990 Camp were: David Scriven (Bosun); John Preece; Alan Preece; Marc Scriven; Wendy Smith; Jim Hemsley; Tony Hammond; Andrew Wooldridge; Neil Harrison; Jon Harrison (no relation to Neil); John Trubshaw and Annie Williams (not Bill's daughter, sadly).

It was a really enjoyable Camp for the most part. There were one or two blips but experience showed, over the years, that such 'fall-outs' were quickly resolved.

It was always nice to receive confirmation that the Camps had been a success, by way of letters from the children or their parents/guardians. Below, however, is a short letter I received from Shropshire County Council Social Services Department following the 1990 Camp. Letters of praise from these organisations are rarer than rocking-horse droppings, so I have treasured this for 27 years:

Dear Mr Scriven
Peter Rudd, and Raymond and Brian Gale thoroughly enjoyed their Longmynd Adventure Camp experience.

Thank you for the effort you and your helpers put in; and I wish you every success for the future.
Yours sincerely
A Griffiths (Social Worker)
30 August 1990.

How lovely, and very much appreciated.
Just prior to Mr Griffiths' correspondence I received this from a friend of our (former) longstanding secretary Pat Hazlehurst:

Dear Skipper
I was very impressed with all your good work at the Camp today. So will you please accept this small gift for your funds; and all my good wishes for your continued success in the future.
Yours sincerely
N V Daley.

This friend of Pat's gifted ten pounds to the Camp. It was always nice to receive such wonderful correspondence; it made all the hard work very worthwhile. And the many kind donations, small and not so small, which the Camp received over the years were vital to its continuing existence. Indeed, those who donated money and/or goods can in no way be separated from the folks who helped us run the actual holiday Camps because without one group or the other the Camp could never have flourished in the way it did back then.

A number of people whom I have been very fortunate to have met through the Longmynd Adventure Camp stick in my mind, for one reason or another.

Owen Lewis was one such character. He was a young, bubbly lad with a mop of 'nearly blond' curly hair; a local Stretton lad whose beginnings of Camp life are recorded in my first book. Owen could always be relied upon for a good story about the locality; like Bill Williams, he was very knowledgeable on matters concerning the Long Mynd and surrounding area. During his years as a helper on Camp, mainly as a tent leader, he worked for Shropshire Radio. He also tried his hand at the performing arts genre. Owen played the harmonica with not a little aplomb, and he was always good for a poem or ditty which he would take pride in reading to us all during our Campfire celebrations. Below is just one such poem I thought worthy of inclusion:

There are many mysteries in the land that we do not understand.
Like why the sea doesn't keep advancing, drowning all the land.
Or how at night, when all is black; the glow worm lights its glowing back.
Or how the moon can look so big; and great big oaks grow from the twig.
There's beer that's drawn from casks of wood. It tastes so

sweet, and looks so good.

And breezes blowing from the hill; that kiss the sick, and cure the ill.

Lots of sheep that jump and play, but never sleep at the break of day.

How the power of flight keeps the birds on high through miles and miles of open sky.

How water grants the angler's wish, by bringing forth the silver fish.

Yes, all these mysteries in the land are things that we cannot understand.

But take a step; watch each day...

And see they happen anyway!

I was fortunate to meet many good people during my time with the charity. Some remained for a good few years whilst others came and went rather fleetingly but most gave us their best, and whatever time they could offer.

I thought it was a real shame that Malcolm Webster (mentioned earlier) felt it necessary to call it a day when he did. But it was a choice he made with his job as a teacher being one of the main reasons, so we wished him well with a heavy heart.

Don and Eileen Mansell were good friends of our Skipper and both helped out on many Camps during the early years. Don as a tent leader, whilst Eileen did the cooking. She didn't suffer fools gladly but was a lovely lady. And Don was never without a smile on his face.

We had many cooks over the years; all of them worth a mention. Being able to feed so many people such good food, daily, with what they had to work with would, I imagine, be in excess of most folks' capability. The closest I came to cooking the food was doing my stints as a "washer-upper" when it was our turn to do the 'Cook's Washing Up' duty, both as a boy and a member of the field staff.

Winnie Hull, the WVS lady, did the job excellently for a number of years during the early Camps. She was the cook when I first went to Camp with my brothers and close friends from Low Hill. Win was a native of Yorkshire but had moved down to Wolverhampton. A really wonderful lady, loved by us all.

Roy Williams was a constant helper at Camp for over a quarter of a century. His wife Di also gave her assistance to Bill whenever she could. This very amiable couple always worked in the kitchen, and gave their very best at all times.

But the one who will be best remembered as the Cook, certainly from 1981 until the middle of the 1990s, is my personal friend John Preece. John was an absolute master at putting quality food on our tables, at the lowest possible cost. A qualified butcher and chef, he certainly knew his trade. To this day, John Preece cooks for me and a few of my former tent leaders whenever we 'set sail' for a few days camping in Minton Batch.

After John, and until the end of my time with this wonderful charity, the kitchen became the responsibility of Wendy Smith.

It has to be said, however, that the person appointed 'second in command' in the kitchen certainly made the cook's job much easier, especially in the case of John Preece. In all my time on Camp, John was the only one who managed to get out of the kitchen during the day, every day! The reason he was able to do this was down to the work ethic of his assistants. John's main helpers during his years as cook were two A1 campers, Dean Nightingale and my brother, David Scriven.

Pat Irvine and her policeman husband Brian, both of Church Stretton, were regular helpers during the sixties and seventies. Pat always helped Eileen Mansell in the cookhouse whilst Brian, a really happy sort of bloke who I liked a lot, was a very good tent leader.

A lot of the boys also stick in my mind. Over the years we had many sets of brothers who benefitted from Bill's kind generosity, as the charity progressed steadily. Some from the 1960s included the Bradley boys - Colin and Robert; David and Terry Hogg ('Monster' and 'Monsterkin' respectively); the Badger brothers, and the very mischievous Locke brothers (nicknamed Padlock and Crooklock).

Ted Challinor, the old farmer from Minton who, along with his father-in-law Jack Williams, allowed Bill to set up Camp on his land from 1963 until 1979 paid us a visit one warm sunny afternoon and, unusually for Ted, he wasn't very happy! Apparently, two brothers from the Birmingham area had let down the large rear tyres of one of his tractors. Naturally, Bill was very annoyed upon hearing this. The initial concession was to offer to pay for the tractor to be put back to full working order, but Ted refused to accept this gesture from our Skipper. Instead, he asked Bill to make the lads apologise to him personally so that he could say his piece afterwards. Bill agreed immediately and the little scamps were summoned to the Skipper's quarters to face the music. Following Ted's departure, the whole Camp was addressed by the Skipper with regard to behavioural standards, especially when off-site. Obviously, a severe deduction in precious tent marks for the brothers' group did nothing to endear them to their mates under canvas. It's a hard life, learning lessons... but very beneficial in the long run.

When occasionally questioned by members of staff as to why a particular boy was at Camp, for example if they had heard that a lad had already had a holiday, Bill Williams would respond: 'Don't always believe what you hear, especially from children who might be trying to shield their poor existence back home.' As a child on Camp I never thought it necessary to try and hide my life back home, and neither did anyone else for that matter. We were pretty much all in the same boat, and we knew it!

When I became Skipper in 1990, I followed Bill's path. I trusted the WRVS and Social Services to select boys for the reason(s) outlined above. My main 'collaborator' on the WRVS (Shropshire) side was a lovely lady called Kim Harris. Kim had a good positive outlook on life; and a bubbly personality which was infectious. I always looked forward to Kim's regular appearances during the actual Camps; always accompanied by her equally charming husband, Gordon. In fact, I would have loved to have had both on my staff but alas, that particular dream never materialised.

Quite early on in my tenure as Skipper I received the following letter from Kim with regard to our policy of not accepting "Young Offenders" at Camp:

Dear Alan

Keith Hoggart (Social Worker) has suggested to me a young lad whom he would like to include on this year's holiday list. He has been to Camp previously, and by all accounts was well behaved. He is, however, a 'young offender'. What do you think? I've told Keith that the Camp isn't suitable for YOs; but as you know the lad, I'd ask you anyway.

Please let me know asap about this lad.

Although the LAC committee didn't meddle (as a rule) in actual Camp policy, I decided (because this would be a major shift in our conditions for acceptance of children) to reply negatively to Kim's letter, pending a discussion on the matter with our chair, Barrie Gretton. We decided to stick to the status quo; so it was a definite 'no' to Keith's request.

I duly informed Kim of our decision, which she graciously accepted, even saying that this would reinforce our policy; even if a boy had been to Camp before offending, he would be disqualified from future selection. This policy would no doubt be frowned upon in today's society but one has to remember that the vast majority of our staff were simply volunteers with little or no experience in dealing with this type of problem. The same went for children with mental or physical problems because we, as a unit, were not cut out for dealing with matters of this nature, unfortunate though it was.

A few days after this I received a letter from Eileen Gahan (Children's Holiday Organiser, West Midlands) advising that forty boys from her catchment would be attending the 1991 Camp. Enclosed in the envelope was a cheque for £1000, by way of sponsorship for the lads.

There were always opportunities for good, reliable people to help with the running of the Camps. It was policy that any fresh volunteer should come recommended by an existing helper, and more often than not this worked out well. One such volunteer was a lovely girl called Nicola Piggott, who initially worked on the 1991 Camp.

Here is Nicky's delightful account of her 'initiation':

Ahoy me Hearties!

I had been to 'the site' previously, to view the quiet and remote fenced-off field, seemingly miles from anywhere; and here I was, less than a week later, making a similar journey... I must be mad!!

But I told myself that I was coming to enjoy myself. And that, believe it or not, is exactly what I did.

I arrived full of fear and anticipation of what lay ahead for me over the next ten days. The 'fear', however, was soon transformed into responsibility filled with fun, love and care.

And I can honestly say that this was the BEST ten days of my life!

The Camp is run on similar lines to a ship, with a Skipper at the helm; a Bosun just below him; a QM (Quarter Master), and a Cook in the galley. Everyone 'on board' is a "shipmate", relying upon, and helping each other.

Camp started on the previous evening, with a small party being held in the hall to offer thanks to everyone who had in whatever capacity helped to ensure this year's Camp took place. It was a chance for me, and anyone else new to this wonderful place, to meet committee members and others who worked behind the scenes, to keep the ship afloat and sailing. As well, us staff members could get together (now that the Camp was ready for the boys' arrival on the following afternoon) to form friendships that would be relied on heavily during the next ten days.

We all rose quite late the following morning; this though, would be a luxury never to happen again during Camp! A hearty breakfast preceded the wait. Then at approximately 1400hrs the fun began! Forty-nine excited on board 'shipmates' (it quickly felt like ninety-four) were ready to set sail on a ten day "voyage". We all enjoyed a fairly smooth crossing - you might say - with many adventures along the way.

Six intrepid groups of explorers, each with its own leader (I was head of Cabin 6) covered the sheer heights of the 'Stretton Hills'; dammed off the white waters cascading down the valleys into the brook which runs the length of Minton Batch. We had many long 'voyages' over the beautiful countryside hills; one to search (successfully) for the lesser-spotted 'whifflepoof' (your imagination is required here please).

We were very fortunate (?) to be at Camp on the only night of the year (the first Saturday in August) when the ghosts of Sir Buckley Minton Beddoes and the "Lady" Lucy Lamplight meet on a bridge in the batch. A scary (because we actually witnessed this) but most rewarding adventure that ensured we all scurried quickly off to our beds after a nice supper of hot soup and bread.

Another 'voyage' we all thoroughly enjoyed was a trip by coach to Towyn, mid Wales. Here we plunged carefree into the sea; made huge sandcastles; played ball games on the beach, and ate fish and chips and ice-cream just like typical holiday-makers. And then, at the end of a brilliant day, we set sail for the return journey to Camp, all of us very tired; but not so much that we couldn't all join in with a great sing-song led by the Skipper and the Bosun.

Every single day was rewarding, with a variety of fantastic experiences. The children and us leaders and helpers all very much enjoyed our time together; bonds were built between all on board. And the looks on each face as the boys left us for home is a sight I will never forget. Every picture tells a story; this one was unmistakenly telling us what a brilliant holiday these lads had enjoyed. It was all we needed to know... no thanks necessary!

I would like to express my grateful thanks to all the people who, in whatever way, help to organise these much needed holidays, which have been an ongoing success for many years. Nicola Piggott (Cabin 6).

Nicola joined us in 1991, and stayed the course. She was a brilliant cabin leader whom everyone thought the world of; not least, the writer.

Nicky mentions the people behind the scenes, and quite rightly. The Camps were successful due in part to the many souls who worked year-round to ensure the 'end product' was successful. And during my time as Skipper I coaxed the committee to regularly attend get-togethers at Camp, where WRVS personnel would be invited to join us for lunch (almost always expertly put

154

on by John Preece).

Kim Harris told me about some of the things that were done year-round in order to ensure their continued sponsorship of a "Shropshire Lad" ... or a dozen, invariably.

I received the following correspondence (dated 26th May 1992) from Kim regarding one of our get-togethers:

Dear Alan

Thanks for your letter. Yes, we are busy, things are really hotting up. Thank you for the 12 places (boys) we have been given; and one extra, thanks to Eileen Gahan (Area Organiser). It's a good job I'm not superstitious (touch wood).

I mentioned your kind offer of lunch at Camp to the team; there may be as many as eight of us! Will this be a problem? Valerie, who represents the Wem and Whitchurch district would have to bring her children along, as she is a single parent. The children have also helped with our fund-raising. I can bring food if required? Please let me know.

See you soon

Kind regards

Kim Harris

A most enjoyable lunch took place on 12th July 1992.

Unfortunately, our day with the ladies of the WRVS preceded the worst Camp we ever experienced! One of the lads brought with him a stomach bug which we gave two nicknames to: the

Aztec Two-step; and Montezuma's Revenge. This unfortunate episode is documented in detail in my first book so I won't say much now, except to offer again my sincere thanks to all my staff on that fated Camp. Everyone put both hands to the pump (so to speak) in a sterling effort to keep the ship from sinking.

Eileen Gahan, West Midlands Holiday Organiser for the WRVS, said in her letter dated 10th August 1992:

I am so sorry that almost everyone was struck down with 'an upset stomach'. It must have taken heroic efforts on the part of the staff to keep the Camp going.

Bang on, Mrs Gahan!

The bug of 1992 served at least to illustrate to us all on the committee that the existing toilet block was no longer fit for purpose. To this end another fundraising project was launched immediately. The aim was to have a vastly improved 'sanitation facility' by the time Camp 1993 rolled round. In early 1993 the *Shropshire Star* published an article about this:

Camp keeps on fundraising for new toilets

A south Shropshire adventure camp is facing a race against time to get its new toilet block finished.

The Longmynd Adventure Camp is aiming to raise £20,000 to pay for the new facilities – and so far £13,000 is already in the kitty. This includes £1,300 raised through an evening of entertainment at Telford Snooker Club in Oakengates, organised by employees of the Midland Red Bus Co.

The 'Skipper' of the Camp, Alan Scriven (himself a Midland Red employee) said, "The night was a huge success – the people we need to thank are too numerous to mention.

"But we still need another £7,000 to complete the new building. We have already gone ahead and demolished the old toilet block.

"We have built a new independent facility housing more toilets... and showers... but we badly need the remaining money for the materials required to complete it."

Alan, who has been with the Camp (as man and boy) since 1965, thanked all the people who have already donated both cash and materials toward the project.

By the time we set up Camp '93 we had our toilet and shower block ready for use, although still not fully completed. But all in good time we managed to see the task done, thanks to the many people and organisations who assisted us in all sorts of ways.

That year's Camp proved to be a massive improvement. Well, it could hardly fail to be!

The Importance of Local Support

A fact that Bill Williams was always conscious of, and drummed into his voluntary staff members, was that the continued success of the Camp depended largely on the ongoing support of the locals. I would therefore like to dedicate this short chapter to the families of the locality, who not only gave their blessing to the Camp's being but also helped it in many different ways to blossom.

Brian and Mary Jones of Minton Oaks Farm allowed Bill to hold his very first, and the second, Camp on their land. They also very kindly repeated this generous act in 1962 and again in 1981, though on a different field from the first two years.

Jack Williams and Ted Challinor of Minton Hamlet supported Bill's early Camps by allowing him to use their land from the very early 1960s, right through to 1979 when we acquired our own small piece of "heaven".

The 1980s began with us holding our first Camps on our very own field; purchased at a very good price from Ned and Clifford Davies, of Minton Batch.

As well as these generous displays of kindness, there was much valued help and support from other members of the local community, too.

Chris Foulkes and his mother proved a constant source of

support to Bill, and later to me. As well as many other acts of generosity, they gave Bill permission to use their field opposite the Camp as a car park during the 25th anniversary celebrations in 1983. I found that whatever form of help we asked Chris for, he always responded positively. Many of the people who made up the community have now passed on, including Mrs Foulkes, but the help and support these real country folk willingly gave to the Camp will never be forgotten by us (in the way we have been forgotten by the people responsible for the charity today!).

The individual families of Minton Hamlet and the surrounding areas supported the Camp in different ways: bringing us cakes and other foodstuff; donating raffle prizes for our 'First Night' parties (which they all attended), and – in the case of the late Councillor and Mrs Lloyd of Acre Batch, All Stretton, and Mr Pat Greenhous of Little Stretton – permission to make use of their outdoor swimming pool.

The ongoing support of the local community was absolutely paramount to the Camp's success. Yes, we could have continued without it, possibly. But we were so much better, undoubtedly, with it! And to ensure, as far as we could, that their support remained constant, Bill and, later, I drummed into the lads the importance of best behaviour whilst out and about. To this end we succeeded by and large because during my thirty-three years with the Camp there were hardly any complaints from our neighbours about the children.

Francis Rudge joined Bill's team of helpers during the early years of its WVS existence; and was a godsend! Fran, like Bill, could persuade anyone to give (or at least loan) us anything. In Bill's case, I think it was due to him being the local bobby; with Francis, the fact that he was a well-known member of the community. Whatever the reason, it worked.

Dave Davies (son of the late Ned Davies of Minton Batch Farm) and Chris Foulkes remain good friends with John Preece and me to this day; twenty years after our association with the Camp ceased. We still camp in the batch every year with a few friends, all former LAC staff members (this place gets in your blood), and Dave and Chris are always there for us, whenever we need their help... which is regularly. We try to repay them in the only way we can, really; by keeping an eye on their livestock when we're in the area.

I'm not familiar with the names of all members of the community but that doesn't in any way diminish our gratitude to all who in whatever way helped us; quite possibly more than they knew.

The Women's Voluntary Service

This book would not be complete without the inclusion of a few words about the Women's Voluntary Service (which became the Women's Royal Voluntary Service and then the Royal Voluntary Service) because without it the Longmynd Adventure Camp, and many other worthwhile charities, may not have got off the ground, perhaps not even with the good intentions of people like Bill Williams BEM and others born under the same brilliant star. The enthusiasm and commitment of all the ladies I came to know from this fine and well-respected organisation was second to none, always. And I am deeply indebted, especially to Kim Harris and Diane Hogg (of the Shropshire and West Midlands branches, respectively) for the help and support they gave me during my time at the helm.

Mrs Marjorie Lathe was the Children's Holiday Organiser for my part of the world. She was a very nice, though formidable, lady who knew her 'job', and did it very well. I liked her very much, and so did my mother. Not only did Mrs Lathe give my brothers and I (and later my sister Carmel) the chance of a very first holiday, she also kept in touch with Mom throughout the months between Camps, helping her with clothing us, etc.

Mrs Eileen Gahan was the accepted "boss" (at least as far as we were concerned) of the Birmingham branch during my time as Skipper in the 1990s. I have little or no information of the "Brummies" prior to this period, with the exception of the soon-forgotten rivalry between the two groups of boys in the sixties.

Thanks to Mrs Pricilla Roscoe and Mrs Kim Harris for kindly furnishing me with the appropriate information regarding the original history of the WRVS, and also some insight into its Shropshire Branch.

Nationally, the WVS came into being in 1938. The then Home Secretary, Sir Samuel Hoare, enlisted the help of Stella, the Dowager Lady Reading, to recruit women to assist local authorities with Air Raid Precautions. He believed, quite rightly as it turned out, that she had the character, vision and organisational skills for such a task. Her response was so good that by the end of 1938 the WVS had a membership of a staggering 300,000.

The general remit was to enrol women to help the war effort and slowly but surely the WVS got its teeth into every aspect of it. You name it, the WVS was involved somewhere.

At the time war was declared, on 3rd September 1939, the organisation was known as the WVS for Civil Defence and was at the forefront of many projects and activities to assist the war effort. In September 1945 its efforts during wartime were rewarded when the Home Office announced that the WVS should continue for 'possibly TWO more years'. What a wise decision it proved to be!

In 1946 Lady Boyne retired as Shropshire County Organiser, and was succeeded by the tireless Mrs Martin Wilson, whose commitment and sterling work brought progress for Shropshire on a scale not previously matched. All manner of schemes and projects were sprouting up, like Meals on Wheels in 1947; delivering hot meals to people who were confined to their homes. A little while later, a mobile library service (arising as a result of requests to the Meals on Wheels teams) was provided for the housebound in Shrewsbury, Wellington and Shifnal.

When the National Health Service came into being in 1948, the opinion of many was that hospital volunteers would no longer be necessary. It soon became clear, however, that this was not so and the WVS actually extended its services to include making and mending clothes to help the nurses, and running the popular 'trolley shops'.

1951 saw the "WVS Roll of Honour" introduced. A memorial to the 241 WVS volunteers killed in the war began a three-month tour of the UK. In December, a Dedication Service at Westminster Abbey was attended by HM Queen Elizabeth who, along with the Queen Mother, was a joint patron.

1959, the year that the WVS Boys Camp (which became the Longmynd Adventure Camp) began in earnest, was also the 21st anniversary of the WVS. There were countless celebrations, including a garden party at Buckingham Palace, hosted by the Queen, whilst the Queen Mother attended a service at Westminster Abbey.

Wartime Prime Minister Winston Churchill died on 24th January 1965 and during the lying-in-state, long queues formed in the bitterly cold streets around Westminster Hall and the 'Food Flying Squad' staffed by the WVS dispensed hot drinks to approximately 82,300 people among the slow-moving crowds.

The Queen in 1966 awarded the WVS the great honour of adding 'Royal' to its title. Westminster Abbey was the venue for a service to mark the occasion for some 2,000 members.

The sixties rolled into the seventies and the now WRVS continued to grow into a valuable and ever progressive existence. But in May 1971, Lady Reading died. Mrs Frances Clode CBE was appointed Chair. She held this position until 1974 when she was succeeded by Baroness Pike of Melton, who in her turn was replaced by Dame Barbara Shenfield in 1981. In 1988, the year of the organisation's Golden Jubilee, the Honourable Mrs Mary Corsar became Chairman (as the term was back then).

Wellington Urban District Council purchased Portway House in 1957 and Parville House the following year. These were transferred to the WVS, which assumed the responsibility of renting the flat-lets created in the houses to elderly people. Bridgnorth Borough acquired a house for a similar purpose in 1960. Children in a position to benefit from the WVS were helped in three ways:

There were "Godmother" and "uncle and aunt" schemes created in county council children's homes. Garments were knitted for such children, with wool supplied by the Children's Department. Holiday homes were provided for Birmingham children – seventeen homes in 1953 – until 1959. Then 200 children from the Midlands industrial areas were given holidays in that August. Of these, 160 were put into private homes; **the remainder went to a camp for boys,** and there was another camp for teenage girls. During this time, depots were distributing welfare foods to expectant mothers and those with young children.

The clothing work, so active during wartime, continued into the peace and several bases were involved with this. Also, vast amounts of clothing were sorted, cleaned, baled and despatched to victims of civil disaster, and war refugees in many parts of the world.

Trolley shops continued to be a welcome feature of hospital life, and at county council homes in Shropshire, with the WVS visitors supplying the needs of patients once a week. A Hospital Car Service supplemented the vehicles of the Ambulance Service. The WVS certainly played its part, and how; with many people benefitting.

In April 1960 the WVS came of age in Shropshire and a 21st anniversary service was held at St Chad's church in Shrewsbury. The Bishop of Lichfield officiated, and the service included a procession of several hundred members.

The Children's Holiday Scheme in Shropshire prospered, with more and more kids benefitting from kindly country homes.

Robin Hazlerigg was to become a WVS 'stalwart' for her tireless work and enthusiasm for a basic campsite set up by a police constable in South Shropshire. Mrs Hazlerigg worked closely with Bill Williams to ensure as far as possible the continued progress of what came to be known as the "WVS Boys Camp". Her and Bill's ability to work together quickly produced a successful friendship, with a dual ambition for the Camp's continued existence.

My memory of early holidays at Camp strongly features the 'dynamic duo' of Mrs Hazlerigg and Mrs Lathe. Both fully dedicated to ensuring the children they selected to go to Camp had everything they needed, including a bit of spending money if their families were in dire straits, which my family for one often were. It was, however, Mrs Hazlerigg who spent time with Bill Williams at actual Camps; even arriving on the final morning of our holiday, and not only to help Bill set the accounts straight but invariably to muck in with the washing up, and general sorting.

The Meals on Wheels operation was so successful in Shropshire that in 1965 there were more schemes in progress than any other comparable county, with 41 members serving between 80,000 and 90,000 meals each year.

By way of recognition of the invaluable work carried out by members, a Long Service medal was struck in 1961 (for 15 years).

The initial outbreak of the foot-and-mouth epidemic occurred in Oswestry market in 1967 and led to sustained demand on WVS volunteers who assisted the teams of veterinary surgeons, and many other folk who assisted in the grim task of containing the disease.

As the years rolled on through the seventies and into the eighties it became apparent that changing social conditions were making it noticeably more difficult to recruit volunteers to replace the ageing; and this problem was by no means restricted to the WRVS. By and large, however, the wide range of social works which had been built up during and after the war continued unabated. This was noted and celebrated at several public functions, and on the occasion of the Golden Jubilee celebrations in 1988.

Cmdr Pilling, chair of Ludlow Rural District Council, observed at a large meeting in the town in 1982: "The main purpose of the WRVS is to make happy the elderly, the under-privileged [as the term was back then], and the disabled; and this is all done through voluntary efforts."

The year 1985 saw the Hospital Car Service (which had flourished for twenty years) taken over by Shropshire Ambulance Association. The number of patients transported this way had increased from 804 in 1962 to 13,251 in 1984.

Children's holidays also flourished, within private homes and **adventure camps** in the Shropshire hills. The clothing service made good progress, too (my family benefitted from the

Wolverhampton branch).

The Red House in Priorslee was acquired by the WRVS in 1985, and quickly converted into flat-lets.

Canteens and trolleys continued to improve life for hospital patients, with WRVS ladies being welcomed at Telford's fine new Princess Royal Hospital in 1990, when membership of the Shropshire WRVS stood at 2,500.

From the early nineties it was evident that the Service was not keeping pace with social movement. Its public image, premises and equipment all required upgrading and in order to do this new funds would have to be found. A review of the organisation by Sir Philip Woodfield recommended changes in the management structure and the adoption of a self-funding system to augment the Home Office grant.

Outside the Service, the introduction of new regulations led to basic reform procedures within it (which ultimately affected the Longmynd Adventure Camp towards the end of the decade). Health and social care underwent a transformation, resulting in the WRVS becoming fully accountable.

A self-funding method was then adopted, with pro-rata contributions from every project. The WRVS became a limited company and its entire structure was reorganised.

The Service introduced a new logo together with a "Vision" statement which expressed future policy:

The members of the WRVS, in partnership with the public and private sectors, are committed to being the premier providers of voluntary assistance to those in need of care within their local communities.

The WRVS was reorganised as a charity, and all accounts were to be subject to national audit. Also, it grouped its work under five headings: Emergency Services; Food; Hospital; Family, and Services Welfare.

In 1991, Mrs Patricia Wilding BEM retired as WRVS transport organiser after twenty-eight years. Under her guidance, volunteers had ferried children with specific needs, as well as disabled adults and the elderly, to school, clinic and hospital.

Deprived children continued to enjoy camps at Minton on the Long Mynd, courtesy of the WRVS sponsorship; and the willing souls who gave their time and whatever assistance they could, completely voluntarily.

In 1990, sadly the final year of Bill Williams' tenure at the helm, I was appointed Skipper, after meeting a number of conditions set by the charity's committee. The most important one, without doubt, was that I secured the ongoing support of the WRVS, our chief sponsor. I spoke with the Children's Holiday Organisers for the counties of West Midlands and Shropshire, by telephone originally, then later face-to-face. I was very happy that the WRVS agreed to continue their unswerving support.

The Women's Voluntary Service

More than anything, I wanted Bill to return... even if it meant finishing with the Camp myself. I don't honestly think it would have come to that, but the possibility had to be recognised. So the continued support of the WRVS was paramount to the Camp's continuity, and the hopeful return of its founder.

Below are a few words from Kim Harris. I asked Kim for her memories of the time she was Children's Holiday Organiser.

These memories are a little (!) hazy because I didn't keep any of the paperwork from back then.

I believe the Birmingham CHO (Eileen Gahan) was our regional organiser, and that our policies etc. were generated from there, although I also attended meetings in Worcester.

I was allocated children's holiday in Lichfield (choir school); Derby (which I seem to remember was hosted by Endeavour Training volunteers); Stanton, in the Cotswolds (hosted by Cheltenham University PE sports students); Oswestry (a church group), and of course, the Longmynd Adventure Camp.

Some input came from Manchester [Manchester was to have a major say in WRVS Holiday policy in the fullness of time] *but I did not attend any meetings there.*

In addition to the camping holidays I also organised caravan holidays for girls and boys who perhaps would not have been able to manage without the support of their families because of disability; health problems, or if they were too young to attend a camp. I rented 'Robert House' adopted caravans (the residential arm of what used to be the Robert Clive School). I also rented Greenacres at Blackrock Sands, Porthmadog; and a site in Fleetwood, near Blackpool... the name escapes me.

I held my position as CHO for seven years, and still remember the moment when I realised – with a jolt – that I was not only responsible for finding the children (usually via Social Services); 'vetting' them for suitability for a camping holiday; sourcing clothes for the ones that didn't have many; arranging the transport, which meant hiring a minibus (thankfully WRVS made one available) and a driver, and escort; visiting the children midway through their holiday, and to be available if a child needed to go home early... but also TO RAISE THE MONEY TO PAY FOR IT ALL!

Thankfully I only had to do all of the above for just a few children during my first year. I began the fundraising by de-cluttering our house; taking all the "treasure" to car boot sales. Then, in an effort to widen my scope, I attended local fetes and carnivals, operating tombolas (the most popular times doing this was when the prizes were Trolls!

I couldn't possibly have done any of the above without the solid support of my husband Gordon, and his mum.

Once I got the hang of the probable cost of each holiday, I knew that if I wanted to do more, I needed to get better at raising money, and would also need more volunteers including minibus drivers.

I heard about a computer programme called (if memory serves) 'Fund a Finder' which I could access at the Community Council Offices. I also found out that the library had a number of (very large) books about Trusts and Charities. All I had to do was find the trusts and charities that had an interest in child welfare; the most well-known of these was of course Children in Need. My good friend Terry Meredith helped me with writing to the various trusts and charities, and with driving.

My fondest memory of those days was receiving a letter from a small charity saying they thought my project was "lovely". They also enclosed a cheque for £2,000.

I also applied to the local Round Table and Lions charities.

Then, came the dreaded LRF (Local Resources Funding). I had to give 5% of every penny I raised to the WRVS!

I had absolutely no idea that the ladies of this fine organisation had to raise the money themselves so that kids could come to our Camp for a holiday. I took it for granted, because nothing was ever said at the time. I take my hat off to Kim, and to all those like her who worked so hard to ensure we could give the children selected a bloody good time at Camp which they wouldn't forget in a hurry. And to the likes of Gordon Harris and his mother who volunteered their help for nothing more than a "thank you", which wasn't even required.

Official Secrets and Official Positions

I celebrated my 40th birthday in July 1993. The staff very kindly clubbed together to buy me a card, which cost (I know this because they left the price ticket on it) a massive fifty-five pence! But it's the thought that counts. And this was evident from some of the comments written within:

Alan Preece: *Never-mind Al' it's easier going downhill... and it's downhill ALL THE WAY NOW MATE!*

Steff Latewood: *Happy birthday O ancient one!*

Nicola Piggott: *Life begins at forty... so I'm told. Is that inches; centimetres..................or MILLIMETRES?????*
  I took it she meant my waistline!

On the front of the card was written: *It's your 40th Birthday just treat it as another hurdle in life...*
And on the inside: *... as long as you can still get your LEG OVER!*
All good fun!

Fun was, for the most time, what Camp was all about. The lads had plenty of it, and so did the staff, between themselves and

173

of course with the boys. We had a chap called Kevin Smith on Camp 1993. He wasn't the brightest button in the bag but very willing, if not always able. One day Alan Preece and I paid a visit to Barrie Gretton at his business premises. Kevin was with us but I can't remember why. He was a tent leader so there must have been a reason why he was with us and not his group. Anyway, as we pulled into Barrie's yard in Dorrington, near Shrewsbury, Kevin said, "What's this place, Skipper?"

Faster than light, Alan said, 'We can't say a lot about his place Kev, or why we're here. But if you're spotted, we could get into deep shit.'

'Cowin' 'ell; why, Bosun?' asked Kevin, obviously shocked by Alan's quick-fire announcement.

At that very instant, Barrie's wife Sue came to greet us from the office.

I said to Alan, 'Come on, mate,' before turning to Kevin and telling him to stay put in the minibus and not to move a muscle. We approached Sue (a lovely lady) and asked where Barrie was. We were told he'd had to pop into Shrewsbury. Sue apologised on Barrie's behalf and told us he would come to Camp as soon as he could. We politely refused Sue's offer of a cup of tea, but asked her to play along with the stitch-up we had started with Kevin. Sue agreed. Alan and I quickly came up with a wind-up before going back to the bus.

'Right,' said Alan to Kevin, who was growing more edgy by the second.

'What, mate?' Kevin said, looking first at Alan then at me. Alan told him that Sue was a military officer, and Kevin, because he was now on military property (even though he'd never stepped foot out of the front of the minibus) would have to sign the Official Secrets Act because of what he had seen whilst on military-owned land. Kevin tried, feebly, to protest; saying he'd seen nothing secret except all the building products on view (in Barrie's yard).

Alan was having none of it. 'You'll sign the form, Kevin, or you'll be interviewed under caution by this lady's commanding officer. Your choice, but I reckon Skip won't be too impressed if you bring the Camp into disrepute. It'll be all over the national press; the BBC and ITV.'

Kevin looked at me but I completely ignored him as I said to Sue, 'We'll have the document drawn up, Madam. This young man will sign it and my Bosun will deliver it to you.'

Sue didn't comment, just nodded her head in agreement. Alan and I got into the cab and we pulled out of the yard with stern, straight faces. All the way back to Camp, despite Kevin's constant comments of concern, we didn't utter a single word. When we arrived I told Kevin not to say anything to anyone on Camp about where we'd been; and to report to my caravan in one hour.

When Kevin duly reported to me, he was asked to sign the following:

SECRET ARMS DEPOT: SHROPSHIRE

02 August 1993

OATH

By allegiance to HM Queen Elizabeth II (Her heirs) and the government of the day; any day and every day I KEVIN SMITH, tent leader on the Longmynd Adventure Camp; swear (regularly) to obey my Sovereign Liege (oh and my Skipper and Bosun); and to uphold her wishes and commands (and those of my Skipper and Bosun) to the full.

I swear that for the protection and benefit of the military forces Commander in Chief (oh, and my Skipper and Bosun) and our Sovereign state, I shall not under any circumstances reveal or divulge any such information which would be beneficial to the enemies of my Sovereign and my country... and my Skipper and Bosun who took me to a place of high security today.

I have also been advised that the ultimate penalty still applies in this country for treason.

I sign on this second day of August in the year one thousand nine hundred and ninety three.

Kevin Smith

Young Kevin, bless him, signed the "official document" without asking a single question EVEN after we asked him to read it out loud twice before putting pen to paper. This off-the-cuff humour caused the whole staffroom to erupt in laughter when later, after the lads had retired to bed, Alan read it out and Kevin still didn't get the wind-up, until a couple of the leaders made him see it. Great fun; and no-one was safe from the wind-ups at Camp; senior staff included... sometimes!

All the banter ensured, by and large, a happy Camp.

During Camp 1995 Alan Preece, whom I had restored to the position of Bosun, attempted to keep secret from the rest of the Camp the fact that he had gone 'AWOL'. In reality I had asked Alan (who very sadly passed away in 2015) to perform an important errand. His very short absence was noticed immediately by some of the boys and a rumour of sorts grew, after another member of staff put it about that Alan had run off to another Camp down the road. The only other 'camp' anywhere near us was the Manor Adventure Camp, which had kindly extended an invitation for our boys to join them for a day on previous occasions. The rumour changed to an opinion when a little later the boys were told that the Bosun had got muddled up with which of the two Adventure Camps he was supposed to be at... and at this moment in time he was obviously at the wrong one!! A meeting with me was demanded by boys and staff alike (these funny little episodes were what our Camp was all about). So bowing to the excessive "pressure", mainly from the staff, I agreed to speak on the matter in three hours' time. This would take us through to our main meal time which was, on that particular day, scheduled for 1900 hours.

The appointed time duly arrived and all the Camp members, with the obvious exception of the Bosun, congregated in the hall. I walked in at exactly 7pm to a rousing round of applause. And then chants of "We want Bosun... we want Bosun..."

I let this continue for a short while before raising both arms. The hall fell silent. And then I began explaining the reason for Alan's apparent disappearance. I remember starting a cock-and-bull story about receiving a note from Manor Adventure Camp saying how our Bosun was enjoying himself at our neighbour's premises. The lads started ranting their disapproval, and shouting suggestions of how we might go there and kidnap him. As all this was going on at great volume, the Bosun walked into the hall, from the kitchen end. Again, the room fell silent. Alan was holding a piece of A4 white paper, folded once. He came and stood next to me as I feigned shock at seeing him.

'Where have you been, Bosun?' I asked him, in a very demanding and authoritative manner. Alan said nothing as he handed me the piece of paper. I scanned the room for the tent staff, gesturing for them to quieten the lads down. Then I held the note out in front of me and pretended to read it with shock and disbelief. After a short period of total silence, with the Bosun standing before us all in a sheepish, butter-wouldn't-melt kind of pose, I announced to everyone that the Bosun had, apparently, been very poorly and confined to his sleeping bag.

The note Alan handed to me was on LAC letterhead. And on it he had cleverly written a "Doctor's Certificate", covering his period of illness (or time away from Camp). Below is an exact copy of the document:

SICK NOTE

Name of Patient: Bosun

Address: Longmynd Adventure Camp, Church Stretton, Salop.

Details of Debility: Feeling under the weather due to Guard Duty.

Quack's Diagnosis: [three lines of squiggles]

Has medication been prescribed: YES

What Medication: Tea in bed and a very long lie-in

When Will Patient Be Fit to Resume Duty: Just after his lie-in.

Bosun was examined by his local hospital VOLUNTARILY! They called in a psychiatrist immediately. And following a thorough brain examination, the following conclusion was arrived at: Nuts; Bonkers; off his head; out of his tiny mind; three sandwiches short of a picnic.An X-ray revealed the extent of damage to the brain over the period of time this man has spent at Camp... He is 100% off his trolley! When it became obvious that he was actually HAPPY about going to this Camp the hospital concluded that there was no known cure for this very strange and alarming behaviour. The problem he has left us with however... is ... How to stop ourselves from repeatedly singing as one; "There's a Worm at the Bottom of the Garden"; and "The Goat Went over the Mountain".

I read every word of this 'masterpiece' out loud, to the delight of all the children. When I finished I asked the Camp what we should do about the Bosun's reason, nay excuse, for his disappearance. To a man, they all supported our Bosun, bless them. That bit of fun, and others like it, were pure gold dust to us who had to keep the place going happily day after day.

So the Bosun lost no "privileges" (whatever they might be) and retained his official position.

I was very happy with my decision to restore Alan as Bosun. He knew the role as it should be played; as I had done from 1980 to 1989. He had his critics, as we all have, but he was the man for the job

Steff Latewood, whom I had chosen to take the position the previous year, was a great guy to have on Camp and I always very much appreciated his help and support. There was no harsh criticism of him in my decision to revert back to Alan. It was simply that Alan was a better fit for that particular job. Some are of the opinion that everything happens for a reason. I count myself among their number. Restoring my late friend to the official position of my number two, I hope, helped the committee to suppose that he was the right man to replace yours truly in 1996 after more "fall-out" from the continued war of words between me and Bill Williams.

Mrs H M Hazlehurst (Pat) QPM was a major and important part of the Camp from its inception until 1996, when she died at the age of eighty-three. Pat was an original member of the committee and occupied the official position of secretary for many years. As well as this, Pat was also, for a good few years, the Camp's cook. And believe me this very formidable lady took no prisoners as she worked tirelessly to put good, wholesome food on our plates.

On Thursday 16th June 1994 Jo Robathan wrote an article in the *Shrewsbury Chronicle* about Pat's distinguished career in the Shropshire police force. As a small tribute for all she did for our "little piece of heaven" I would like to offer the reader (with the kind permission of Shropshire Newspapers Ltd) a few excerpts from Jo's wonderful article which also included two photographs: one of Pat during the early 1950s, pounding the beat as a sergeant in High Street, Shrewsbury; and the second one showing her in the company of eighteen male members of the police federation (Pat represented female officers).

How things have changed
since Pat became a Pc

The long arm of the law has always been a force to be reckoned with, and according to Pat Hazlehurst, so it should be. Mrs Hazlehurst became Shropshire's first detective constable in the 1950s. Her career spanned twenty-five years and saw the creation of the West Mercia Police Force. She retired in 1973 (same year as the Camp's Founder, Bill Williams BEM) just one year before male and female officers were integrated and women gained full pay. Born in Worcester and brought up in Lichfield, Pat was the daughter of a civil servant. When her family moved to Shrewsbury Pat followed and took a job as a civil servant in the Army Pay and Records Office. After meeting her husband Jack Hazlehurst, a sergeant in the North Staffordshire Regiment, the couple married in February 1940.

Pat was working part-time in an accountant's office when she was told her husband had been killed at the 1944 Battle of Caen in France. He was 30. [We at Camp were led to believe that Pat was widowed only a few months after her marriage. No-one ever asked her about this.] *She had to leave Army married quarters and took a job as manageress of a small Shrewsbury hotel owned by some acquaintances. It was here that she got talking to a policeman who suggested she joined the police force.*

Pat said: "In those days it was considered a job rather than a career but I joined in order to get a job that was interesting." After a three-month basic training course... she became a Pc at Wellington. She spent two years at Wellington...

She then became the first woman in Shropshire to be sent to detective training school at Wakefield... She was posted to Swan Hill as a detective constable earning £8 per week, and that was the start of the happiest part of her career...

After four years in the service Pat was entitled to take her sergeant's exam. She passed in 1953 and returned to uniform, her "fear of God" suit. Although a sergeant, she had no authority over the men because policewomen still had a separate department but she did have overall supervision of the female officers...

At this time there was no establishment for a female inspector in Shropshire, but nevertheless Pat took her inspector's exam in 1956... she found herself, in 1964, with the job of inspector... Her rise through the ranks was not yet complete – she was promoted to superintendent and posted to West Mercia HQ at Hindlip Hall in Worcester...

On her retirement Pat was awarded the Queen's Police Medal for Distinguished Service. She has travelled to Trinidad, Canada, Cyprus and Malta and has devoted much of her time to the Abbeyfields Society which provides homes for active elderly people.

Pat also spends a great deal of time with The Longmynd Adventure Camp for deprived children in Church Stretton; and the British Legion Poppy Appeal.

What a fitting tribute to a very nice lady.

Now, here's another ditty from Owen Lewis, penned on 25th July 1996, and spoken as is The Lord's Prayer:

Our leader, who art in the staffroom; whatever be your name. Your kingdom's Camp; your will, will be done on Camp as you would in Minton. Give us each day our daily bread, and forgive us when we trespass as we forgive those who trespass against *us. Lead us not into Marshbrook, and deliver us from Ludlow, for thine is the Camp plan; the power and the glory. The heather forever, Amen!*

***

By the time the middle nineties were upon us my official position as Skipper of the Camp was about to be taken from me... albeit for just one Camp. It came about via the saddest episode in this charity's thirty-seven-year history, all fully documented in my first book.

At this time my official status as far as my private life was concerned was 'divorced'. I had in fact gone from being a single person to being married, then divorced again, between September 1993 and December 1995. Following this I vowed never to get so involved with a woman so quickly again... and I've kept true to that promise to myself.

In my working life, I was a duty clerk at Midland Red Bus Company, at its Wellington depot. I know it's only a coincidence but I loved the fact that my mentor in life, Bill Williams, hailed from Wellington, and began his twenty-five-year career in the police force in this lovely little town in Shropshire. And here I was myself now working in Wellington.

Bill was now Managing Director of his own security bus'ness, based in Shrewsbury. Before our fall-out I used to do a bit of canvassing for him around the Shrewsbury area; sometimes also in Wolverhampton. This was when he started his very first home security business from his own home in Meole Brace, Shrewsbury, in the mid-eighties.

On 13th October 1994 Bill was the subject of a column in the *Shrewsbury Chronicle*. The writer of the piece was Jo Robathan, who had penned the article on Pat Hazlehurst a few months earlier. The report on Bill covered his life to date and also listed a Q&A section. Here are a few that Jo lists:

Q: What person has influenced you the most?
Bill: My English teacher at Wellington Grammar School.

Q: How do you relax?
Bill: The only relaxation I ever get is walking on the Long Mynd, and I don't do as much as I should. The Long Mynd is my favourite place.

Q: If you were on a desert island what three luxuries would you choose?
Bill: A few books, a tape of Under Milk Wood *by Dylan Thomas and my multi-purpose woodworker.*

Q: What are your earliest memories?
Bill: When I was five and my father died and I wasn't allowed

to go to his funeral, venting my anger on a bucket of water which I kicked as far as it would go.

Q: What is your greatest fear?
Bill: I'm not a good swimmer so my greatest fear is drowning.

Q: What is your favourite film?
Bill: Lady and the Tramp. I saw it a long, long time ago when it first came out, and I thoroughly enjoyed it.

Q: What is your favourite book?
Bill: The one that sticks out is Wind in the Willows which I remember from childhood. But I have more a love for poetry than stories. I don't have a lot of time for reading these days.

Q: If you won £1million how would you spend it?
Bill: I would probably expand my business; and look after the family.

Q: How do you spend your Sundays?
Bill: Gardening; walking; reading the Sunday Telegraph, watching television.

A wonderful insight into the mind of this great man. I well remember our walks on the Long Mynd, year round, with Terry Pugh. Terry was even more of a shadow to Bill than I was, especially during my early years as part of the Camp. And I've no doubt that he loved Bill as much as I did.

Terry and Bill had been friends since Bill created Wistanstow Youth Club. He was always at Camp, with no particular responsibilities except a bit of driving as required. A good bloke was Terry, one of the best, along with a few other early 'personalities' of Camp such as Pete Roberts, Mick Powell, Brian Irvine, Don Mansell, Chris Toolan, Richard Lewis, Mrs Hull and Roy "Butcher" Williams.

For the 1996 Camps I was known as "Scriv" (my accepted nickname). I was asked to lead Tent Two, and was allocated a great group of lads who worked well together, and became friends quickly.

One of my campers was a Shrewsbury lad called Mathew Pritchard, and I have no doubt that had the original format of the Longmynd Adventure Camp continued after 1997 this kid would have made a brilliant tent leader. He could be left on his own to organise the tent and fellow occupants for tent inspections, and litter competitions, etc., whilst I was absent on other business with the Skipper and/or the Bosun; and he always succeeded. Matt kept in touch with me throughout the year by letter. I received the following correspondence from him after telling him that I had been reinstalled as Skipper for next year (1997):

Dear Scriv (Skipper)

Thanks for your letter; it was nice to hear from you again. I'm glad you got your job as Skipper back. I really hope I can come back to Camp again, and so does Philip.

I hope being Skipper doesn't stop you from playing football with us. Please say hi to Tom and Marc for me.

Remember, I said we would win the tent competition from the third day, and we did!

Hope to see you all again next year.

Matthew Pritchard (Tent 2)

After serving my sentence for crimes committed against the committee by writing to Bill Williams on LAC letterhead paper in 1996, I was reinstated as Skipper for Camps 1997; although I have little doubt that this decision was taken with 'heavy heart' as far as some, if not all, of my committee colleagues were concerned. But on the positive side, here I was, back at the helm. This year the two Camps, each shorter than the usual ten days, were the fiftieth and fifty-first. The reasons for two shorter Camps as opposed to one ten-day event were, one: to mark the charity's fiftieth Camp, and two: to offer the same number as we would have if we'd stuck to the one ten-day Camp. The programme was re-styled slightly to accommodate Rhyl Sun Centre (suggested by Shropshire WRVS), which proved a wrong move to say the least! The details of this disaster are included in my first book.

But much more important issues were surfacing. Not least the fact that as things stood, after the two Camps ended we were essentially cut adrift by our current sponsors, following the withdrawal of Shropshire WRVS's interest. All our hopes were now fixed on the north; Rochdale and Greater Manchester.

The year's Camps passed into the LAC's history quietly. No-one joined us for our fiftieth celebrations, except Bill Williams. I was so happy to see him sweep through the gate to, as it turned out, Skipper the Camp again, albeit for just this one day; his presence more than made up for everyone else's absence. Naturally, I tried my very best to coax him into returning properly, but to no avail, sadly. Bill reiterated his decision not to become involved again (at any great length, anyway), in a letter to the then committee secretary Don Rogers. Don had written to Bill on 31st January 1998, asking if he would like to become part of a small sub-committee being formed, to organise the LAC's fortieth anniversary in August.

Bill replied on 10th February. Here is an excerpt of his letter:

Dear Don

Thank you for your letter regarding the proposed 40th year celebration of the Camp. I am very interested and would be glad to help in some way. However, you will be aware of the manner of ceasing to be involved with the Camp, and although people's interpretation of the situation at the time may be different, one thing is certain; I was to say the least, extremely *hurt and angry.*

With the passage of time I have found myself able to forgive what I considered to be a great injustice. But I cannot forget. I have made a positive decision not to become involved again with the Camp, although I shall always have the interest of its continuance and expansion at heart.

Bill finishes his letter by suggesting that he and Don get together for a drink to discuss ideas, etc. Whether that came to fruition or not, I do not know.

Between Bill's letter and the proposed dates of the forthcoming fifty-second Camp we (the committee) had decided to revert to one ten-day event. The writing was on the wall, however. I had tried to point this out to the committee but to me there appeared to be a hint (at least) of apathy. My first book contains all the sad details which forced the cancellation of our most important milestone so I won't dwell on it now. It was a most poignant and depressing time for me personally, because my mind kept drifting back to 1989/90 and 1996. I believed, and still do today, that it was largely my fault that we were now in this worsening mess. I've always maintained that my decisions of 1989 and subsequently 1990 were the right ones at that time, but even so, they remain regrettable. As for my stupidity in 1996; well, there are no excuses!

The majority of children who had come to Camp in 1997 were

expecting to be invited back again. They had no idea what was happening to a place they had known briefly but loved immediately. I did, however, write to Craig Heselwood to let him know of my decision to step down as 'Skipper' after he had contacted me earlier to say he was looking forward to seeing me "next time". Craig replied on 10th June 1998:

Dear Skipper
Is it alright if I still call you "Skipper"? Thanks for your letter, but I broke my heart when you said you're not Skipper anymore, and when you said you might not see us anymore. I started crying. You were the best one there. If I ever go to Camp again I will be thinking of you. I will let you know when I am there and you can come and visit us, please.

So sorry you're not Skipper anymore. I will keep writing to you.
Yours faithfully
Craig Heselwood (Heywood, Lancs).

That reply from Craig had the same effect on me as mine had on him. I am still in touch with Craig. He is now a serving police officer, having realised an ambition he had set himself since being a child on Camp, and I am very proud of him. Craig wrote me a very nice letter on 9th Aug 1997. I include it below because his words echo those of many lads who had come to Camp over the preceding forty years:

Dear Skipper

Thank you very much for being an excellent Skipper; you did an excellent job. The "trip" was altogether very good, but you made it that bit better, so I think you deserve this special letter. You all did a very good job, but you did the best of them all.

When I got home my mum said did you have a good time. I said "Mum if I could go back again I would be first in line because the staff were so brilliant."

I would like to come back as a leader to help you.

I am also writing to 'Bosun', and Neil my tent leader.

Thanks again Skip. I will miss you very much.

When my decision to end my time as Skipper became known to all members of the committee, Wendy Smith, who was also a member of my staff at Camp, wrote me a beautiful letter, which also brought a tear or two. A few excerpts below:

Dear Alan

Your resignation makes me so sad. You have been a part of the Camp for most of your life, in one way or another; and no-one else has seen the changes you have witnessed year after year. Some for the better, but some just recently, we can't feel are for the better because we have difficulty understanding them...

Our saving grace is that we have people like you around, with a wealth of first-hand experience and skill, who devote part of their time to helping children...

Unfortunately, more and more of us are giving up because it is an uphill climb against those with the law on their side...

Alan, if it is all this red tape that has made you resign, then let me just say this. As a Camp we cannot change the basics of what we do, nor do we want to. The vast majority of the children we look after enjoy the Camp as it is; we only have to see their tears on that last morning to know this. And whatever happens regarding the way the law stands, the law cannot stop us loving what we do; giving kids the holiday they so obviously want.

I realise that you carry the added burden that should anything go wrong, you are the one in the firing line. But Alan, surely you don't think that we would let you take the bullets on your own...

The committee is the same as any other; it has an important and necessary role in any organisation. But it is detached somewhat from the realities of the Camp because 'their' involvement is limited. The children ARE THE CAMP. The leaders and helpers do whatever is needed; but YOU are the one who holds it all together!

I see, as do many others, how you captivate them all on that very first day, and you hold them for the duration of the Camp. And I find it very difficult to think who could do that as well as you do. It is hard work, and a lot of responsibility for you, but what in life these days, isn't...

Please rethink your decision Alan; the place just wouldn't be the same without you.

Love, Wendy X

I appreciated both letters enormously. But my mind was made up; I saw it as the end of the road for the Camp as we knew it. A completely voluntary organisation had been swallowed up by the ever-rolling wheels of progress, health and safety, and, dare I say, political correctness.

I didn't possess the qualifications obviously required to satisfy our new sponsors at WRVS Manchester. Honest hard work, dedication, experience and commitment counted for nothing... or at least not a lot!

I simply did my job on Camp, whatever it was, during the previous thirty years as a helper, under (for the most time) the direction and leadership of the late great Bill Williams BEM.

It wasn't as if we held no regard for change; or indeed having the continued health and safety of the children AND the staff at the forefront of our thoughts. The following document was designed after my meeting with Mr Hirst. It never saw the light of day, however.

Longmynd Adventure Camp
DISCLOSURE OR DISCOVERY OF ABUSE

It is the duty of all staff to prevent abuse to the children and to report any abuse suspected or discovered. This should be reported at once to senior leadership of the Camp.

At no time should any member of staff put themselves in a one-to-one situation with a child.

Although we are all volunteers, we still have a duty to the children under the Health and Safety at Work Act 1992.

The following declaration must be read and signed in the presence of the Camp leadership; and will be treated as strictly confidential:

I certify that I have no convictions for criminal offences against children; neither spent nor pending.

I have been made aware that the work I am volunteering for will be with children, and therefore exempt under the Rehabilitation of Offenders Act 1974. Any and all previous convictions against children must be declared.

Signed
Name
Address and contact no.

Okay, maybe not a proper legal document, but enough to put off perhaps any unwanted offers of 'help'. I know and accept that we had been very lucky with our selection of helpers over the life of the Camp. And I also knew where our sponsors were coming from regarding their concerns. After all, should anything untoward happen, their necks would be on the block as well as ours... or mine, as Camp Leader. All I was asking for at the meeting in Manchester (described in my first book) was a little time in order to satisfy their demands. Our fortieth anniversary was almost upon us when Mr Hirst, the WRVS Children's Holiday Organiser put his non-bending conditions (or demands) to me. And that, coupled with the totally 'lethargic' response from my colleagues on our committee helped me to realise and accept that not only had the 'wall' been built but the writing was well and truly upon it, clearly! The Longmynd Adventure Camp was finished in its original format, which it had been operated under so successfully for forty years! It was a cruel blow, I thought, even taking Mr Hirst's conditions into consideration. It was cruel because the Camp deserved at the very least a celebration of its achievement to date. And it **could** have happened but for the total disinterest from the people one would have expected to be behind it...

The minutes of the committee meeting held at the Camp on Monday 20th July 1998, after I had formally resigned as Skipper, included the following quote:

Alan explained his reasons once again for his belief that the Camp could not continue in the present format. The committee generally agreed with the situation.

Shortly after this, as news of my resignation reached more and more friends and associates of Camp, I received a nice card from Nicky Piggott. Below are parts of my reply to her kind gesture:

Dear Nicky,

Many thanks for your card, it was very nice of you; and I appreciate everything you said... I sat and thought, as I read it, what Camp has brought to my life over the last 33yrs; and the many friends I have made as a result... I hope the "do-gooders" realise the anguish they have caused by calling time on our style and format which was so successful. And our record for the most time was impeccable.

I could have continued I suppose, as a 'puppet Skipper' but that's not me, as the people who really know me will verify. Better in the fullness of time to go now I think knowing that we had the best years of this wonderful place. I feel no real bitterness towards anyone. And I'm honoured to have achieved so much from an adventure which really, should have only lasted a maximum of four years, when I was a child.

I intend to resign my position on the committee shortly.

Thank you for all your help and support over the last seven years. Please keep in touch. Love, Alan x

As the reality of what had unfolded became ever clearer, all the feelings of guilt and betrayal towards Bill repeatedly visited my thoughts. I was in no doubt at all that this mess was, at least in part, down to me.

I wrote the following letter to Bill on 30th March 1999 after spending some time with him at his home. I'd told him I was considering writing the history of the Camp. He was in agreement, and even gave me everything he had on the Camp, i.e. committee minutes, and other very useful documents. I wish now that I could have finished writing the Camp's story whilst the great man was still with us.

Dear Bill

It was lovely to see you again today; and Debbie too. I really look forward to sharing time with you whenever we can do so. I wanted to say thank you again for the items you kindly gave me to assist me in writing the Camp's history. Looking through the minute book, I came across a letter you received recently from Don Rogers, enquiring if you would be willing to play a part in the forthcoming anniversary celebrations. The letter had your reply attached, and I have to confess to reading both. The first paragraph of your letter touched me; all the hurt you were put through nine years ago has returned again to haunt me.

I know, and you certainly know that at the end of the day, I played my part in it all, and I would never try to excuse myself, and lay blame elsewhere. But as I've said before Bill, I honestly thought I was doing right by the Camp. Whatever anyone else may think, I never intended to run the Camp instead of you; after you, yes. And that was what we were both working so well together for up until that night at Camp in 1989.

I would have willingly stepped aside – or even out of the picture altogether – if you had returned, and wanted that.

You are aware of how much I tried to contact you throughout the dark years. But why should you have spoken to me? I betrayed you, I know. I'm so very sorry Bill. Me "going with the flow" so to speak, rather than trying to see through it, or talk to you first, has without doubt in my opinion, had massive repercussions on the Camp. What I mean is, had you still been at the helm, there's no way the Camp would be in this mess now. You would not have allowed the 'red tape' to "strangle" us. Yes, I accept and agree that some changes were needed. It's just so heart-breaking that we weren't given the time to see this year out first before a thorough over-all of our policies and format could be agreed with our main sponsors, the WRVS.

The second paragraph of your reply to DR mentions the passing of time, and how you can now forgive, but not forget. I appreciate that Bill because neither can I. Every time I see you it all comes flooding back; and frequently the tears flow freely, because what happened to you was a travesty; and I'm deeply ashamed of myself for every minute of hurt it caused you and your family.

If you cast your mind back to that "committee meeting" or what passed for one in the caravan at Camp at the back end of 1989 when a 'secret ballot' was held, I actually told you which way I'd be voting if you continued to refuse to discuss the reason(s) you yourself had summoned us to the Camp for. It wasn't a set-up Bill; I give you my word on that. I promise with all my heart that I had no clue as to how the others would vote. Each made their own decision.

I still believed, before the ensuing meeting at Judge Northcote's place in March of the following year, that it would all be sorted favourably, even though there had been no contact at all between you and I.

But now Bill I want you to know, and hopefully believe, that all the Camps I led from 1990 to now; I would have willingly sacrificed every single one of them, to work just ONE with you again! Obviously, it's too late now for both of us (and that's a crying shame in itself) and this just compounds all the feelings of guilt that keep stirring inside me.

I like to think I made a success of my time at Camp; we had some truly great and memorable times didn't we? And it was never the same without you Bill, not ever.

I'm not looking to try and discard the 'overcoat of guilt' which I have been forced to wear by my own hand, over a body racked with shame, because these feelings will never leave me. As you rightly say; one cannot forget.

But that said Bill, I am grateful for your forgiveness; more

than I can say. You are the one person in the world whom I respect the most. You treated me like a son from 1965. And I have loved you as a father since my first Camp. Thank you Bill for EVERYTHING! See you again very soon.
Best Wishes always.
Alan

I returned Don's letter and Bill's reply with my letter, but Bill sent them back to me, saying he meant to include them. Not to be spiteful but hopefully, he said, to confirm to me his forgiveness. What a great man.

In July 2000, I nominated Bill for the so-called 'People's Awards'. Below are the final few words of the nomination:

All too often we see, or hear of "celebrities" honoured for their charitable efforts. The PEOPLE'S AWARD is a real opportunity for us to bestow deserved recognition to the 'unsung heroes' of life, of others less fortunate. No-one gave more than Bill Williams.

To no great surprise (perhaps because Bill wasn't a famous celebrity) I heard nothing in response.

On 5th December 2012, the following article, written by Andy Richardson, was published in the *Shropshire Star*. I include it below, with the above letter in mind:

Future looks bright for adventure centre

Its links between the Black Country and Shropshire stretch back decades. The Longmynd Adventure Camp has welcomed disadvantaged youngsters for many years, in many cases providing inner city youngsters with their first ever taste of the countryside.

Five years ago, the charity faced an uncertain future and was on the brink of closure because of a huge funding shortfall, and mounting bills. Fast forward to the present day and it is thriving, having tripled its number of users.

Earlier this year, the charity met the Queen after winning a Queen's Award for Voluntary Service. And more recently it has won one award and one award nomination from Wolverhampton Wanderers owner Steve Morgan in the Morgan Foundation Entrepreneur Awards.

It's been a remarkable turnaround.

Trustee Kim March said he was delighted that the Longmynd Adventure Camp could look forward to a more certain future. It received its award for 2012 Best Entrepreneurial Charity or Social Enterprise from Steve Morgan during an Oscars-style presentation ceremony at the Carden Park Hotel near Chester, before an audience of 300 guests.

The camp received a £10,000 cheque from Mr Morgan and a further £2,500 when Mr March was named the runner-up in 2012 Best Individual Entrepreneur category.

Honours

Mr March said: "When I looked at the achievements delivered by other finalists I felt genuinely humbled by the honours bestowed by Mr Morgan's Foundation on our small charity.

"The evening was awash with incredible and moving stories of entrepreneurial achievement, some in the face of considerable adversity. Just to be a part of it was a privilege in its own right."

The Longmynd Adventure Camp is one of Shropshire's longest-running charities that benefits young people. It was founded in 1958 by local policeman Bill Williams when he and his late wife provided a week-long holiday for disadvantaged children. In the space of a year, a single tent in the back garden of the police house grew into a camp for 26 Black Country boys on the Long Mynd.

During the 1970s, the organisation worked with the Women's Voluntary Service in Shrewsbury and Wolverhampton to create two one-week camps for more than 70 boys.

The camp later acquired a field in Hamperley and then in 2006 extended its use from two-weeks-per-year to 33-weeks-per-year. Five years ago it faced closure due to a lack of refurbishment funding but it has enjoyed dramatically improved fortunes.

It is managed and maintained by a dedicated group of volunteers and its primary aim is to provide free or subsidised respite breaks for disadvantaged children, particularly those that have never previously enjoyed the countryside.

The organisation does not receive any regular funding from the Government or local councils and it lets the facility to recognised child welfare, educational, social and vocational groups. Some of its income goes towards the cost of accommodating disadvantaged children from Shropshire, Wolverhampton and other parts of the Black Country and the West Midlands.

It has a number of dedicated trustees who volunteer their time, including secretary Kim March, chairman Don Rogers and treasurer Malcolm Hoad. In order to win its award from Mr Morgan, it faced down competition from hundreds of candidates from Merseyside, Cheshire, Shropshire, North Wales and Wolverhampton.

Mr March added: "There were seven award categories. It is quite unusual for any organisation to make the finalists' short list in more than one category in any one year."

Judges recognised the camp's five-year journey from the brink of closure to that of a revitalised model voluntary group with a long term future. The journey includes the major landmarks of raising £130,000 to refurbish and extend the camp's 30-year-old buildings and raising the camp's profile with a near zero budget.

Mr March said: "It's entirely vocationally-driven as a Church Stretton-based community initiative."

The money received from Mr Morgan has come at exactly the

right time and will be spent meeting tough new European Union water quality standards.

Mr March said: "The camp is located on the eastern flanks of the Long Mynd and has enjoyed a good water supply from the South Shropshire Hills-fed borehole for more than 30 years.

"New regulations, however, which were issued in 2010, do not apply to individual residences with a private water supply unless they offer a commercial accommodation service such as Bed and Breakfast. The camp is judged to fall under the new, demanding EU standards and the trustees have little choice but to dig deep to comply with them."

Mr March added that the Camp was busier than ever providing places for unfunded deserving children, particularly during the present age of austerity. Don Rogers, its chairman, said: "As each year passes I ask myself, 'surely things can't get any better for the Camp, can they?'

"Each year they somehow do, though 2012 will be hugely difficult to top. We were presented to the Queen during Shropshire's Diamond Jubilee celebrations at RAF Cosford and received the award from Mr Morgan. We also have enough funding to bring more rural respite than ever.

"To think we were staring closure in the face in 2007. I'm truly delighted that Kim has had some recognition for delivering on the rejuvenation plan."

There are one or two factual errors in the above report that anyone who has read my first book will realise. But this is an article from 2012, and the book was not published until December 2016. It just shows that the current committee are not in possession of some historical facts.

It's very nice that Don was "truly delighted" for Mr March; and I take my hat off to the man's commitment to the Camp. And it would have been very nice also, if someone on the committee in 2001 could have been "truly delighted" at my appointment with the Queen to be presented with the MBE in recognition of my thirty-three years with the Camp. I believe I'm still the only person connected to the Camp to be honoured in such a way but to this day I have never received one message of congratulations from any one of my former colleagues on the committee; at least two of whom are still serving members.

I also attended the Jubilee function day at Cosford (referred to in the above article) with some members of my family, not knowing of course that the Camp had a stall of sorts there. An 'incident' involving my son Tom and the Camp representatives took place without my knowledge, at the time. This 'incident' caused me sufficient displeasure to decide to relay it to the *Shropshire Star* newspaper by way of a letter (see excerpts below) written on 9th August 2012; which was ignored. The letter began with me offering a brief history of my time with the Camp, and the MBE award.

I then got to the nitty gritty of my reason for writing to them:

My son approached the LAC stand at the Queen's Pageant at Cosford on 12 July. He mentioned to Malcolm Hoad that his father (me, not Malcolm's) had been awarded the MBE for his voluntary service to the Longmynd Adventure Camp. Mr Hoad said: "Who's your dad?"

I remain the only person to date to receive the MBE for service to the Longmynd Adventure Camp, but Mr Hoad didn't even at least acknowledge that fact, even though we both served on the committee at the same time, before I finished.

When my son told him my name, Mr Hoad said "Just a minute," then made his way across the stand to where Mr Don Rogers was stood. Tom knows Mr Rogers from his own time as a member of staff on the Camp. They spoke together for a while before completely ignoring my son.

Tom came and found me wandering about in the hangar, and told me what had transpired at the LAC stand. He also handed me a copy of the Dawn Chorus, *an apparently new LAC editorial he had picked up off the stand whilst waiting (in vain) for Mr Hoad to return. Much of the comments regarding the Camp's early history are factually incorrect, as are the dates of the photographs etc.*

My name; and service to the Camp didn't even get a mention, and hasn't since. This isn't a case of "sour grapes". I have been, and remain very humble about my award; never once using it for my own gain. That said, however, I am very proud of what I achieved with the Camp; from being a boy enjoying holidays, to my years of dedicated voluntary service. Even taking charge in 1979 after Mr Williams, our founder was taken ill.

Mr Rogers is pictured on the front of the Dawn Chorus *receiving on behalf of the LAC the 'Queen's Award for Voluntary Service'. Apparently it is the "MBE for Voluntary Groups".*

Cheers Don.

As I said above, the *Shropshire Star* elected not to publish, which I accept is its right.

Moving On

Since my time with the Camp was now over, I had to find other things to occupy me during my summer holidays from work; and in fact, every break I had! Being so used to Camp taking up all my spare time, I immediately found myself at a loose end. Then during the spring of 1999 my friend John Preece came up with a wonderful suggestion which has stood us in good stead ever since. Although our time together at Camp had ended on a somewhat sour note a few years earlier, we had by now become firm friends once more. John suggested that we ask Dave Davies if he had any objection (because he rented the land) to us approaching Mrs Challinor, who still owned most of Minton (including the field Bill set up Camp on from 1963 until 1979), to ask if we could camp in the field behind. It was the one which Bill used to hold our Sports Days on when we were children at Camp. John wanted me to ask Mrs C because he said she knew me right from when I was a child at Camp. I was the only one, he reminded me, who had been a 'constant'; and Mrs C liked me, he said. All this was true of course, but I still didn't fancy actually "taking the bull by the horns", so to speak. I was very reluctant. Not at the idea, but actually going to see Mrs C at her home in Church Stretton. The family had lived on the farm in Minton Hamlet before her husband Ted's passing in 1989. I was worried about us disturbing the old lady, and that she wouldn't know me from Adam if she actually opened the door to me (us). But John, being John, managed to talk me into it.

Mrs Challinor was wonderful! She recognised me almost immediately (well, after I introduced myself properly), and seemed delighted that I was visiting her. John and my son Marc accompanied me; we took her some flowers and a nice box of chocolates for her daughter, Carol. The end result was that we gained the good lady's blessing, which she promised to put in writing. She kept her word, within a fortnight.

We were now "on a mission".

The first thing we had to do was move our small caravan from the LAC's front field. The caravan belonged to John and me so we had no hassle from the committee when I told Barrie (Gretton) that we intended to move it; on the contrary, actually; he/they were glad to see the back of it.

We kept our plans a tight secret; telling only a few of our closest friends and family where we were "relocating" to.

John and I decided to spend two whole weeks of basic camping in the field behind our "field of dreams". I begged the canvas roof (which was due for replacement) of a replica 1920s charabanc based at the Midland Red depot in Wellington, where I worked. That served as a makeshift cover for a garden barbeque which a couple from work had kindly given me. John cooked all our meals on this piece of apparatus. It had seen better days but we were very grateful for it, and everything else that we begged, borrowed or otherwise obtained (to use a phrase made "Camp famous" by Bill Williams back in the day).

That fortnight in 1999 was brilliant. We used our time wisely every day. Rising early each beautiful morning, we made our way down to the brook (through the small field that had served us all so well from 1963 on the western side of the brook until 1979) and washed in its cool, refreshing water, as we had done so many times in the past. Then following a cooked breakfast and a clean-up of the site, then our plans for the day would be debated and agreed. It was usual for us to do the same activity together; we would, though, on occasion go our separate ways before meeting up back at 'camp' for another good meal. Most evenings, weather permitting, were spent outside sitting by a small fire with a can or a glass in my case, John drinking copious amounts of tea. I kept something resembling a diary of our first holiday in that field, and would like to share with the reader some excerpts from it:

Monday 23rd August 1999

I arrived at the caravan at approximately 1300 hours, and set about emptying it of all "outside" items i.e. toilet tent, and tents etc. John arrived at about 1330 hours, and we had a cup of tea.

We then went shopping at Tuffins in Craven Arms, but only after enjoying a meal in the on-site cafe. John, the bastard, *asked the waitress if she could get me a bib, because I was "prone to making a mess". She obliged; much to John's mirth. I ate every bit of my meal wearing that bib. We also had some fun as we did the shopping; taking the piss out of everyone, and making shop girls laugh. On our merry way around the store we bumped into Terry Pugh, a Camp volunteer during all the years Bill was in charge. Tel explained to us that he worked here at Tuffins. After a brief catch-up he turned to us and said: "Ah well, I'll go and clock out, and piss off home. See y' boys." He hasn't changed obviously... except in his appearance. He looked to be in his late fifties easily. Whilst chatting to Terry, he told us that Bill (Williams) was due back from Turkey today.*

Back at Camp we sorted the food out before John made a small fire. We then rigged up the BBQ, and even put a canvas shelter over it (the roof of the charabanc). I erected one of the tents whilst John made long use of the toilet! Later on, we went "rabbiting" with our air-rifle [we only ever took what we would eat... but we both loved rabbit from back in our childhoods]*, but were unlucky. We spotted a lot; but missed more, or John did! The day ended with us sitting beneath the massive old oak tree, in the dark chatting quietly beside the fire with a few cans. Inevitably, the topic of our conversation was the Camp. We were both so happy; privileged even, to still be part of this beautiful countryside now that our time "up the lane" was over.*

Thursday 26th August 1999

Following our main meal of the day which we sat down to at 7pm, we had a stroll up to the telephone box in Minton. As I sat outside whilst John spoke with Sue, thoughts of the countless times I had walked up to this old red box with lads on Camp, visited my mind. We would either have been on the "Scavenge Hunt" on the final Sunday afternoon of Camp, or I would have been escorting boys who wanted to call home or wherever. I very rarely actually used the phone myself.

Sunday 29th August 1999

This evening, we sat around the fire with a beer, chatting for ages about when we were kids on Camp in the next field. I suggested we went and sat in the field just for old time's sake. But John's response was "nah fuck it Scriv, it's gone a bit chilly; maybe tomorrow." I couldn't argue because it had gone noticeably cooler all of a sudden. Perhaps Sir Buckley and the Lady Lucy were knocking about..........?

Once in our sleeping bags John started telling me stories about his time as a 'butcher's boy' at two shops; one in Low Hill, and the other in Fallings Park. It was really interesting because for anyone who doesn't know the ins and outs of the butchery trade, I guarantee they'd be fascinated. It made my tales of being a 'newspaper delivery boy' look like a walk in the park... or down the street! I also worked at two shops, both in Low Hill. Sleep eventually claimed us both.

Monday 30th August 1999

Whilst in Morris's we saw an advert telling of a caravan that was for sale. I rang the seller, who lived in Church Stretton, and after expressing our interest we arranged to have a look at it. It was a bargain at £200.00 so we bought it. This evening John put a couple of rabbits on a slow heat, then we went to meet Maria Mansell, an old friend of ours, Skipper Williams and the Camp. It was good to see her again (bet Dean was sorry he didn't get to see her... well not on this occasion, anyway).

Tuesday 31st August 1999

This afternoon we visited Francis Rudge to return my set of keys to the Camp, but he was out. I decided to post them through his letter box, with a brief note. This evening, after another delicious meal of roast breast of lamb, served with home cooked chips we sat outside by the fire, chatting about our time here in this wonderful little bit of England. The dying embers of the fire caused the small flames to change colour as the field grew darker and darker. We didn't bother making more light; there was no need. We could see all we needed to. Conversation topics varied regularly, as is the norm. When finally we doused the fire and made it all safe; got into our sleeping bags, sleep came quickly for us both.

The remainder of my diary for that first camping holiday after leaving the LAC is missing from my considerable collection of memorabilia. Suffice to say, the final days were just as good as every previous one. We arranged to collect our "new" caravan after getting permission to put it next to our existing one, and that went smoothly. In fact, every time we were there it all went well. And over the years, during our time in that field, a few of our closest friends and family joined us whenever they could.

All good things come to an end, however.

A few years ago, I arrived at the caravans to find a letter nailed to the larger one. It was from a company of estate agents based in Craven Arms. The letter warned me in no uncertain terms that unless I removed my caravans (in a stated amount of time) they would be towed away and destroyed, and I would be billed for the cost of such drastic action! I was fuming!

Dave Davies, the farmer from Minton Batch told me later that he had been given notice, too. Apparently, a relative of Mrs Challinor had now taken over all her business responsibilities, and decided immediately to get rid of our caravans **and** Dave, who up till now, and for many years, had been renting "our field" and others around it. Although I never actually met the author of that spiteful letter, I knew from Dave, who had, that he was a "nasty piece of work".

We both paid the new tenant a visit, but without any success, so John and I decided that as both caravans had "seen better days" we would cut our losses and leave the 'Godfather' (as we called the gentleman from Craven Arms) to remove them at HIS cost! And that is exactly what we did.

Both of the caravans remain there to this day. So it was just spite, pure and simple. The new tenant originally told us he had no problem with us and our vans being in the field. They were discreetly tucked into the hedge and invisible to all but the few who knew they were there. No. It was, apparently, that relative of Mrs C. He was obviously keen to show that he had inherited none of the charitable warmth and kindness that she and her family had shown us from the very early 1960s. John suggested we both visit Mrs Challinor in an effort to reverse, in his words, this pathetic and unnecessary decision, if indeed she had sanctioned our eviction. But that was out of the question as far as I was concerned, for two reasons: If she had given over authority of her affairs to this relative, she would be reluctant to get involved, however much she was happy for us to be in one of her fields. Secondly, she was now resident full-time in a Church Stretton nursing home. It wouldn't be right to go there and potentially cause her any further upset. I say 'further' because with her now being separated from her daughter Carol, she had enough to deal with, bless her.

So with heavy heart we left that field and moved on, to a very nice spot in Minton Batch, courtesy of our friend Dave Davies. By this time a few of our friends from Camp had joined us. It wasn't possible for all of our mates (including family members who had worked on Camp) to spend time with us at our new spot, due to family commitments, etc. But they are always welcome to join us if and when they are able to.

Every cloud has a silver lining, however. The good thing to come out of our enforced move was the fact that we were now camping properly again, which was something we hadn't done since ending our time with the Longmynd Adventure Camp.

For the final few years that we had the caravans, they had become a real luxury. Our friend Steve Phillips, alias "the dude", had used his carpentry skills to convert them; the larger one (that we purchased from that man in Church Stretton) to sleeping quarters, and the small one he expertly converted into a kitchen/diner.

To this day we spend as much time as we possibly can at our new spot in Minton Batch. It seems as if time stands still when we are at our "country residence", but as we all are acutely aware, time and tide wait for no-one.

The new millennium arrived in no time. At this point in my life I was still with Arriva, in the position of traffic manager at Wellington depot. I loved Wellington and the depot itself was a lovely place to work. I know to say we were all a big happy family is a cliché but Wellington did give that feeling, to everyone (or almost everyone) who worked there.

As the days moved ever closer to this momentous occasion I thought about my junior school headmaster, Mr Hull. In my first book I mention that this fine and well-respected gentleman told me and my classmates, back in the early 1960s, that the new millennium was something for us all to look forward to. He said he had no chance of seeing it but if we youngsters looked after ourselves and life was kind to us, we had a fantastic chance of witnessing it. And when it did happen, I shed a tear for Mr Hull; and for the life I had back then.

Big and small businesses were all concerned about the dawn of the new millennium. There was a general fear almost that at the stroke of midnight all the computers would crash, and chaos ensue. I received a telephone call from a senior manager at our head office in Cannock. He asked if I would 'put the feelers out' for a volunteer to stay at the depot on New Year's Eve to keep his/her eye on the computers. John Morrow offered a very large bonus (tax-free) to whoever would agree to give up this massive celebration evening (well, how often does a new year, decade, century, millennium come round? Yes, we all know the answer, just making the point!) to be at the depot.

'Leave it with me, John; I'll get back to you when I've asked around.'

The fact was, however, I had absolutely no intention of "asking around" once he had given me the figure that the incentive was worth. I couldn't just say there and then that I would do it myself because he made the point of saying that I must put it to the drivers first. I'm not proud of myself for what I did next, but the money would come in very useful at that time in my life. What I did was wait a couple of days then I rang John and told him no-one was interested... but if he was stuck I would give up my evening for the good of the company, and for the bonus figure originally offered. John agreed immediately. And on that most important evening, I didn't even stay at the depot. Well... there was no possibility of every computer crashing just because the clock ticked midnight, I considered. And so it came to pass.

One could look at this in two ways: I didn't want to pressure anyone into agreeing. Or that I should have done what was asked of me before offering myself. I hope any of my former colleagues reading this will forgive me; and maybe even thank me for not asking them and putting them on the proverbial spot. But I somehow doubt it!

So the new millennium began without fuss or panic, and everyone got on with their lives. It was announced by our seniors at Arriva that there was to be a "management restructure" which would affect all of us. Nick Newcombe was the general manager at Wellington and he advised me to apply for a 'Passenger Services Manager' position. This was to be the new title for the current depot manager positions. In my own mind I had no chance of success, but he insisted I could do the job. Also, at that time Arriva expected one to apply for any position higher than the one already held. I threw my hat into the ring; the result in May 2000 was my promotion to PSM of Cannock depot. More challenges!

***

John and I continued with our set-up in the old sports field. And one warm, sunny morning after breakfast we were sitting outside the caravan idly chatting when I noticed someone heading straight for us. The hair on this approaching figure's wispy hair was blowing to one side, and whoever it was (because neither John nor I could identify him/her as yet) was clad in a light blue top and swinging a small bag. I grew just a little concerned because our new spot was still a big secret; not many people knew we were here.

'It's a woman, John,' I stated, very confidently. 'Who the bloody hell's this, mate?'

John remained silent right up to the moment when we both realised who it was...

Bill Williams had kept his promise to visit us, and we were both delighted to see him. But of course, John being John, he couldn't resist the opportunity of a laugh. 'Scriv thought you was a woman, Bill; he thought his luck was in as you walked towards us.' Bill laughed out loud, which caused me and John to laugh too. But my fiend, sorry... friend, had succeeded in embarrassing me yet again!

Bill stayed with us all day; it was a brilliant day. After a couple of cups of tea Bill said he fancied a walk "on the Mynd" if we were up for it. I certainly was; the thought brought back instantly all the previous days Bill and I had spent throughout many years, walking, a lot of the times with Terry Pugh, atop this famous old Shropshire landmark. John immediately registered his interest to join us, and he then got up and went into the caravan saying, 'I'll make us all a bit of lunch to take with us, Scriv you can carry it, mate.'

Even back then, for John to equal anything I did regarding the Long Mynd was a fantastic show of guts, determination and positivity. And now, almost two decades later, he is still managing almost everything we do when we are in the valley.

Bill, John and I walked steadily to the top of Packet Stone Hill, via Minton Batch on the Long Mynd; it was just like a scene from *Last of the Summer Wine*.

Bill got into his stride, and began relaying captivating tales of folklore and historical facts about this beautiful spot in South Shropshire, just as he used to do all those years ago when we were all together at the WVS Boys Camp.

It was a memorable day; one I treasure, as I know John does too. Bill only visited us once during our years in that memory-filled field, but it was the best day we spent there.

***

I was growing into my new position at Cannock depot, but I wasn't liked by many of my "colleagues". Apparently, I arrived with a reputation for being a hard and strict manager. In my defence, however, I would say that I was firm but fair. I just wanted to see everyone doing their job properly.

After joining Carvers straight from school, I received some

sound advice from my first ever boss, Mr Jack Biddle, the general manager, who had worked all his adult life at Carvers; starting as a junior warehouseman, as I had. Mr Biddle (I never once addressed him by his Christian name; such was my respect for the man) was second only to Bill Williams as the male influence in my life. He predicted that I would have a successful working career, and he promoted me five times during my eight years with Carvers; I ended my time with the company as warehouse manager. The advice he gave was simple but very important: 'Always listen to the other person's point of view; and never judge without being in full possession of the facts.' I have, throughout the numerous managerial posts I have held over fifty years, always stuck to Mr B's advice. So no, I do not think I was a harsh manager. I simply believe that some of the people I have worked above, and below, only looked at the "mist". They didn't bother to try and see through it!

Whilst sitting at my desk at work on a warm May morning in 2001, I received a call from a lady who identified herself as Pat Cattermole. She told me she was speaking from the cabinet office at number ten Downing Street. To my utter surprise she very calmly advised me that my name had been put forward to Her Majesty, that she might consider me for an award in recognition of my charity work.

I was subsequently awarded the MBE in the Birthday Honours; and duly received the award from the Queen on 6th December at Buckingham Palace. It was a memorable day for me, my sons and my youngest sister.

This wonderful accolade made the local newspapers. The article appeared in the *Cannock Press* on 31st January 2002:

Bus garage boss honour. MBE for services to needy kids

Alan Scriven has received the MBE he was given in the Queen's Birthday Honours List. The 48yr old has, for over thirty years, tirelessly raised funds, and worked voluntarily for the children's charity The Longmynd Adventure Camp. He has tackled the infamous 50 mile Longmynd Hike on a few occasions to enable needy kids to attend the Camp. Neil Barker, managing director of Arriva Midlands North said: "We offer our sincere congratulations to Alan."

Those seven words must have been very difficult for Neil to utter because he and I never again really saw eye to eye after I wrote to him concerning a matter at my then depot, Wellington. I used the phrase "with respect", and it went down like a lead balloon. I said it with genuine respect for him and the position of MD which he had recently been appointed to. But he took it as me taking the piss. And despite my apology (after learning from one of his subordinates his feelings regarding my choice of words) we never experienced anything remotely resembling a good working relationship again. In fact, not long after my appointment with Queen Elizabeth, I was unceremoniously packed off to Shrewsbury depot (the so-called managers' graveyard) as their PSM.

It came to pass not long after my ill-fated transfer to Shrewsbury that the company's hierarchy decided on yet another middle management restructure. But I opted not to join the "circus"; instead I chose redundancy, thus ending my longest spell of continued employment with the same company.

Since leaving my position in Shrewsbury I have remained in the industry, in various positions, including driver, assistant manager, and inspector with Choice Travel (which sold out to D&G Bus and Coach, who in turn sold their Wednesfield depot to Arriva, so I was once again their employee). During the spring of 2016 I got wind that Arriva intended to close the Wednesfield premises and spread the drivers (who couldn't find work elsewhere) around their remaining depots. I wasn't in any way keen to continue working for Arriva so found myself at a forthcoming 'loose end'. Following my involvement, however, in a three-vehicle collision one afternoon in July (for which I was harshly awarded a final written warning), my mind was made up; I was leaving this (in my mind) failing company once and for all, whether I had another job or not!

Luckily, my friend (and former colleague at Wednesfield depot) Simon Harris asked me if I would be interested in joining the small bus company which he and a few others had left Arriva for. I said yes immediately and he gave me the boss's number.

I rang Ben Brown there and then, the result being that I left Arriva (again) on 12th August and after a week's camping in Minton Batch I joined Select Bus Services of Penkridge, Staffordshire, on 22nd August; 531 years (to the day) since the tragic and treacherous murder of the last Plantagenet King of England, Richard III, at Bosworth, Leics. I only include this piece of our history because of my interest in this (in my opinion) much-maligned anointed monarch.

***

Since the new millennium began, a number of good people who gave what they could to the Camp during my years as a senior member of staff, have passed on. I am honoured to pay tribute to them here, in no particular order; and I offer my sincere apologies for anyone I forget to mention: Malcolm Webster, Eileen Mansell, Rita Rogers, Sid Cliffe, Barrie Gretton, Francis Rudge, Terry Pugh, Mrs W F (Hetty) Williams, Mrs H M (Pat) Hazlehurst QPM, Jean Humphries, Judge P Northcote, Mrs P Northcote, Alan Preece; and last but not least, Mr W F (Bill) Williams BEM.

Bill passed away, after a fall, on 14th October 2013. He lies at rest in the churchyard of St Mary's church, in Church Westcote. His funeral took place on Friday 25th October; followed on Monday 28th October by a memorial service at Holy Trinity

Church, Wistanstow, which I attended along with many former colleagues of early Camps, including Pete Roberts, Mick Powell, John Preece, Dean Nightingale, Steve Phillips and the Right Reverend Richard Lewis. Richard also attended and indeed took part in Bill's actual funeral service earlier.

There is a beautiful poem, called *This Life Mattered*, which was adapted from *What Will Matter*, by Michael Josephson. It summed up Bill and his full life, with reference to integrity, compassion and significance. It was sent to me by a friend of mine of many years (thanks to Bill and the Camp) called Lyn; daughter of the late Don and Eileen Mansell of Church Stretton, both valued helpers to Bill during the Camp's early years. The simple note from Lyn which accompanied the poem read:

Alan, here's the poem I promised you. Made me think of Bill (Skipper). Bet you think it, too.

Absolutely, Lyn, Thank you very much.

After Bill's memorial service we all congregated in the Plough pub, a familiar venue for many of us "campers", and Bill's local during his time as the bobby for the area.

I am sure Bill would have been happy with the turnout for his funeral and memorial service; the gathering of his friends and family at the Plough gave us all an opportunity to rekindle old friendships as we discussed times gone by. At the end of that day, a few of us who were with Bill at Camp back in the sixties and seventies agreed to keep in touch with each other. And we have done so; with Ann and Debbie, also.

A short time later we all met up in Little Stretton and ate lunch together as we planned our own celebration (separate from anything the current committee might do) of the Longmynd Adventure Camp's 60th anniversary this year, 2018. Bill always dated the Camp from 1958; and we celebrated the 25th anniversary in 1983, the year Bill was awarded the British Empire Medal.

We do not intend our celebration (which will take place at Camp, after Ann was very kindly granted permission from a member of the committee) as a snub to the people who are currently connected to the Camp. We just wanted to get together for a few days on our own to celebrate the anniversary as well as what the Camp between 1958 and 1998 meant to us.

Boyhood memories

I began this book with some words from the founder of the Camp, Mr Bill Williams BEM. I would like to end my story about the Longmynd Adventure Camp between 1958 and 1998 with the "essay" Bill asked me to write, as part of his own life-story. He wanted to know my inner-most feelings about what I actually thought of the Camp when I first arrived in 1965. It is written through the eyes of me as a twelve-year-old lad having his first experience away from home:

Billy, my older brother, said I'd regret not keeping to our agreement with our newly acquired Rediffusion television set, when I "get to that camp". The year was 1965; Billy and I had been allocated a place at a holiday camp which he'd already been to, the previous year. It was called, apparently, the WVS Boys Camp, but all I knew of it was what he had condescended to tell me, which wasn't a lot but enough to make me ask our mom if I could stay at home. I suggested that David (14 months my junior) could have my place.

"Don't be daft," Mom said, "He's just pulling your leg."

I looked at Billy, and he just shook his head slyly. Needless to say, I relented and let him watch his programme.

When we got our tele Mom was concerned about the possible falling-out between us kids, about what programme we watched. So she allocated us all a day between (and including) Monday and Friday, with herself deciding the weekend's viewing. It was fair enough, I suppose. We could do deals between ourselves on what programme was watched during any evening, so that was okay. Well until I refused, apparently, to stick to a swap agreement.

The letter arrived. It told Mom of our appointment at the WVS offices in Broad Street, Wolverhampton. The organisation subsequently moved down the road a little later, to Fryer Street.

The appointment was arranged so that we could go and get "suitably" rigged out for a ten day "holiday" at the back of beyond! Plimsolls (or pumps to us); wellington boots; shorts; underwear; jumper; t-shirt; socks (although I later found out that we were never allowed to wear any at this place). They also gave us a towel and a coat each, and a brand new pair of blue jeans. As above, with the socks, so it was with the jeans because we were told that shorts were the best way to dress whilst we were at this place.

If you were very lucky you received a brown leather suitcase to carry it all in. I was never that lucky though, so like most of the other lads, my stuff was packed into a couple of brown paper carrier bags.

We had to be at Faulkland Street coach park at 1pm prompt, on the Friday. Mom took me and Billy on the number 3 bus and waited with us until we were safely on the coach. I looked at her through the big window of the coach (it was only the second time I had ever been on one for a long journey), and she waved to us as the coach pulled away. That was very sad for me. I hated leaving her, even to go to school, and knowing for certain I would be back with her later, after school finished. But this day was different! I knew it, and it really hurt me. I kept the tears at bay because of Billy, and all the other kids on the coach; but I could have broken my heart because I loved her so much. I hated being away from my mom. Seeing her face for the last time for nearly two weeks was almost more than I could bear. Billy knew this too, and made the best of it by calling me a "mommy's boy" and laughing. I was dreading this camping place we were now headed for, and it seemed that I was the only one feeling like this. All the other boys; those who got on the coach with us, and the ones already on board when it arrived, were all seemingly happy and glad to be leaving their "home comforts" for a while; but not me!

That journey took forever. Once we were out of town proper, and the hustle and bustle, the scenery became wall to wall countryside that I for one had never seen before. I had heard about the countryside in Nature lessons at school, and seen some pictures in books, but I had never seen it for real. It was massive!

The majority of the lads on board were quite obviously keen to get to this hell-hole my brother had described. They must be off their rockers; that's all I could think.

Eventually, and after what to me seemed like an age, the coach came to a gentle halt. Immediately, the lads who had obviously been to this place before began jumping up and down like a group of demented chimps; shouting out stuff like "There's Skipper!" and "I hope I'm in the same tent again with our leader." One or two said they weren't washing in that cold brook again. Eh... cold brook? So Billy wasn't pulling my leg like Mom said he was!

He was just as bloody enthusiastic as that lot, our Billy. Showing themselves up, and making fools out of each other.

The lady from the WVS who had travelled with us kept asking everybody to sit down and wait for the skipper, whoever that was? Then she said, "Ah, here's Mr Williams now." But all I could see as I looked to my right from my seat on the coach was a group of about ten blokes coming at us with speed from the top of a little hill. And most of them wearing nothing more than a pair of (in most cases) badly fitted shorts. And the one at the front, I noticed as they drew ever nearer to us, was wearing a bleeding knife! Oh my God, I thought to myself, what is this place?

The big man wearing the knife came to the door of the coach, leaving his friends in the field looking at us all and smiling; putting their thumbs up to lads they obviously recognised from last year, or the year before, I don't know. After a short chat with the WVS lady, the big man gave her a little parcel, which

I discovered in due course was a packed lunch for her and the driver for the journey back home. How I wished, at that moment, that I could have gone back with her. But no such luck because at that very moment we were given the go-ahead to get off the coach.

It was mayhem as we all got into the field. Lads were running to these blokes and renewing old friendships; suitcases and carrier bags were hauled out of the underside of the coach as the names of the owners were called out by the driver. Some listened out for their name and picked up the bags or cases that were theirs; Billy and I were in this group. Others simply ignored the driver, leaving the big bloke's mates to fetch them and carry them up to the top of the field. Weather-wise it was a lovely day, but I felt lost and alone, as my brother ran off to join the others, like David Hogg and John Preece, who were dragging their luggage (like him) as they made their way up the field.

It turned out that the big bloke with the knife was the boss, just as I thought. Billy hadn't said anything of any use to me, he was far too interested in his mates to care about my feelings. But it was just so clearly obvious that this man was in charge. His voice was authoritative, and he looked like he was the main man... and I quickly discovered that this was the case when he introduced himself as "the Skipper".

We all moved into another field to the left of us, and I noticed a massive white tent, and a few others close by it. The big man asked us all to sit down on the grass because he wanted to "sort us out". Bloody hell!

We were divided up into groups of five or six; brothers being given the chance to stick together (as me and Billy did) or separate (most stuck together). But, we were told, in no uncertain terms by the Skipper, the decision we made now, sticks; no changing minds afterwards.

We were put into tent number four. The young man who was to be our tent leader was called Hugh Williams. He was no relation to the Skipper, but did have two brothers, and also his dad helping on this Camp. There was an old lady who had also come here on the coach with us, and stayed after it had departed on its return journey. She was introduced as Mrs Hull, and she would be cooking for us, Skipper said.

I was very impressed with our first meal on this Camp. Mrs Hull, with the help of Hugh's dad; a giant of a man, had cooked us a very tasty stew. And we were even given a pudding, like at school. We all sat together in the massive white tent which was called a marquee... apparently. But as if to dampen my slow interest in this place, aided by the delicious grub, we were told by the Skipper, as we ate, that certain "rotas" would be implemented (whatever that meant) as soon as the meal was finished. And true to his word, the Skipper explained the duty rotas and a few more rules and regulations that we would be required to follow. These points were as well as a general overview of the "campsite", and surrounding fields etc. 'Don't *do this, don't do that. Do this, do that'.*

The WVS woman up town told us this was going to be a holiday! Yeah, right.

The field had two rows of tents at the far end; these would be our living space for the ten-day duration. Ours was a smallish one which our leader Hugh explained was a 'bell tent'. It did actually look like a bell, to be fair. Billy and me would be sharing it with George Murray, our friend from down Fifth Avenue; and a lad called Brian Guest who was as new to this as me and George were.

After that first delicious meal some tent groups became involved in Skipper's rota. Washing up all the things used by the cooks, and fetching water from a spring up the narrow lane was all that was needed to do on the first evening.

By now most of us had changed into shorts, and no socks. This was so that if we wanted to play in the brook at the bottom of this field, we wouldn't get soggy socks. Some lads refused point blank to wear shorts (as some of the early photographs show), and their tent group paid the price of losing valuable tent marks. Tent marks were awarded and de-merited as a form of discipline, for various tasks or misdemeanours.

Hugh took our little bit of spending money off us to keep it safe. I was hoping Mom would keep her word and send me and Billy some more cash; sometime next week, she said. But like many of the lads on the Camp with us, no more money came our way, from home; once what we had was spent, that was it.

As the week wore on we all, at some point, visited Doctor Skipper for various reasons, but blisters, from wearing no socks was the main reason.

First evening was spent with Skipper. This was a tradition that lasted for years; right into my time at the helm. He took us for a walk up the valley, telling us weird and wonderful stories as we all clung to him... well us new lads, anyway. The valley was a bit frightening at first; when it got a bit dark, and all sorts of horrible noises – no, not the kids' farting – kept disturbing us (I did grow to love the valley though, and it is still plays a major part in my recreational time). The brook running through it provided endless hours of fun, as did the hills on either side of it. Skipper led us past the farm, and asked us to always stay on the right of the farmhouse, and we always obeyed this request.

Once we were well away from the farm... and the dogs... the Skipper would organise some communal games, like stalking; cowboys and Indians, and ducking contests in the brook. But the all-time favourite valley game was, without any doubt, Harbour Light [and I tell of this fantastic night game in my first book].

I loved all the games we played together as a whole Camp, outdoor and indoor when the weather was wet. Skipper taught us to play The Farmer and the Poacher, British Bulldog, Turks and Russians, and many more. Indoor games included Teacher to John, Who Sir Me Sir, and Forfeits.

On the flip side, we all endured blisters (consequence of no socks until our feet got used to it... on the last day!); washing up; walking miles every day, and of course, kipping on the ground! We had to fetch water from a dribble up the lane, when it was our turn on the rota; humping dirty great logs from here, there and everywhere to keep the cook's fire going. That was a strange one actually, because for the final evening's campfire, Mr Rudge (or Mr Fixit as he came to be known) fetched all the logs we could possibly burn, and more! Oh, and on occasions we even had to empty the bogs. Yes, on bloody holiday!

The cooking fire burned all day long; the smell of the wood smoke was constant, and I loved it.

My first night at the Camp was not something I had been looking forward to. Trying to sleep on the ground, albeit on a wafer-thin bit of something, in a tent you couldn't lock, miles away from home. When it was time for bed Hugh came with us, armed with a small torch no brighter than a match. He 'shone' it around the tent to 'assist' us into 'bed'. Then once we had got into these contraptions we'd been shown by Hugh how to make earlier, off he went; promising to come back before we knew it. We never saw him again till next morning, when he woke us up from his own "posh and proper" sleeping bag. Skipper paid each tent a visit just after the tent leaders had left us, and we all tried to keep him as long as we could. But he'd be off after a couple of minutes, leaving us all alone in the pitch-black darkness, in the middle of nowhere. Thanks Skip, nice one. See you in the morning if nothing comes in and eats us!

*After Hugh and Skipper deserted us we would start to scare one another about "true stories" of what scared us last time we slept out in the open... as if. Ghosts; clowns; monsters, all sorts of nasty night frighteners... then Billy told us about "the mad axe-man", and what he got up to! He **was** real, my brother said. He had seen him whilst up the valley ghost-hunting (it gets worse). Well as he was the only one in this flimsy shelter who had been there before, we believed him. And the ghosts are real too, Billy said. But then, yes; Skipper had told us about the ghosts earlier, in the valley. He said two of them meet on a bridge, he showed us the very bridge, and it wasn't very far away either. Oh Mother, where are you?*

*Oh shit, I need the toilet. Now I've got to try and get out of this bleedin' envelope of a bed, and go out into the dark! "Anybody need the toilet before you go to sleep? I'll come with you if you want." **We all went!***

That first night was terrible; we were all brickin' it, even Billy. We heard noises like you'd never imagine. It was hellish!

*At the end of day two, however, we were glad to struggle into them envelopes. Skipper's remedy for lack of sleep, hence noisy tents, was **walking, lots and lots of walking.** And you know something; the beds became very comfortable as the nights wore on.*

About halfway through my first ever holiday, I began to get used to the place, and I also started to like it. Skipper was a good bloke (for a copper) and treated us all equally with no favourites... even though we all thought we were his favourite.

We travelled about in an old cow-truck, which was almost guaranteed to break down every time we set off. Skipper always managed to fix it, though. He took us to Bridgnorth Boat Race, and we all really enjoyed the day. I remember him telling us that we were nearer to our homes than to Camp as we stood on the river bank. "Which way is it, Skip?" Terry Hogg asked, much to everyone's interest!

One morning after breakfast Skipper showed us a letter (genuine) from Bell-Vue Zoo in Manchester. After reading it out to all of us he posted it on the notice board in the marquee. The people from the zoo (you know what I mean) were asking us to catch a whifflepoof. Skipper told us not to get this animal mixed up with the even lesser-spotted pooflewhiff. He said we were all going to go out later to see if we could get one and send it to the zoo. Some bright spark suggested there was no such thing. Skipper soon put that to bed by describing one to us. Apparently it can travel at speeds up to 90mph whilst asleep! So imagine how fast it would be when awake! Was it ever still, we asked. Skipper said it always rested by hanging upside down in a hawthorn bush. Also, it rested between the hours of 11am and 4pm. Better get a move on, then. One final bit of info; to look at it, it resembled a log of wood, and had spikes that looked like nails. I was looking forward to the hunt; we all were, especially after Skip told us that a lady doctor (Dr Gooch) from Church Stretton was going to treat us all to a nice meal, with chips (we never ever had chips at Camp) afterwards at a cafe in a place called Cardingmill Valley. What he didn't tell us was that we were going to have to walk about five hundred miles over the mountains, looking for this damn whissleproof or whatever it was, first!

Eventually, we managed to catch it. Well er... what we actually "caught" was... a log of wood with nails hammered into it! I, like many of us, couldn't believe that we had done all that walking just for a bit of wood. But if I'm honest, the meal more than made up for it.

On the two Sundays we went to church. The Catholics went first because their service began at 10am; then us C of E'ers. Not going to church wasn't an option; not if you didn't fancy peeling spuds whilst all the others were out of Camp. And it was okay really. Skipper asked us not to imitate demented cattle as he drove us to Wistanstow church in the cow-truck. That request, however, always fell on deaf ears.

Eventually we all got interested in winning the "tent competition". The winners were announced at the end of campfire on the final Sunday evening. The winners received a book (Observer) prize; and in later years, a certificate.

The Camp magazine really took my interest. I wrote lots of articles; even won first prize once. They were sent to our homes a few months or so after Camp, and they never failed to bring back lots of happy memories of the last time we were there.

We had a day of Sporting events against other tents for much valued (by now) tent marks. They were held in the field behind the one we camped in, and I really enjoyed the day. After all the varied field and track events, such as high jump; egg and spoon; 3 legged; obstacle; 100yds; 200yds and 400yds had been completed we did the relay race. And then, after a short rest, we all, or nearly all, took part in the gruelling cross-country race. The route took us out of the bottom gate, then up the lane into Minton. We then had to run through the middle of the hamlet before turning left and walking (well not many of us could run) up the hill, and along the top. We could see the Camp in miniature below us; even Skipper sitting at his table waiting for us to arrive back at Camp. Going down the hill was a nightmare; high bracken and stinging nettles everywhere. But once you got to the bottom, it was a nice easy stroll (unless you were among the front runners hoping to win the race) along the batch and back into Camp. Skipper put members of staff along the route to count us and help keep us safe. It worked too because there were no problems at all. Once you were checked in, it was down the brook for a wash. And it was needed too, after that gruelling steeplechase!

We had a day at the seaside, and it was brilliant. It was Borth we went to in 1965. We just found a patch on the beach and stayed there all day, except for an hour or so to go with Hugh and spend a couple of bob... if we had any money left. And it was a big if!

Almost as soon as we got going, Skipper stood in the aisle and got us all singing camp songs. This would come in useful for the Campfire at the end of Camp because singing songs was a big part of the evening. After a great day out we boarded the coach about sixish for the return journey. More singing for those who hadn't fallen asleep and before we knew it we were at Newtown. Here was a chance to use the toilets and take advantage of Skipper's generosity. He kindly treated us all to pop and crisps before we set off on the second and final leg of our journey. Skipper played his mouth organ brilliantly, and we sang along; fantastic.

I was getting to love this place. I had got used to the dark nights, and most of the 'duties'.

*There was only one snag about my first trip to the seaside. Skipper copped me (well he **was** a copper y'know) wearing welligogs (wellington boots, to the uninitiated).*

Back at Camp Mr Rudge had lit the Tilley lamps in the marquee for us. We were given a supper of hot cocoa then bed. What bliss; a lovely end to a truly fantastic, exhausting day. Thanks, Skip.

The second Saturday was busy and exciting. Anyone who had any pocket money left could go into town after breakfast and spend it on presents for the family; or themselves if they wished. One or two lads opted to keep what they had left for when they got back home.

Following lunch (which was usually sandwiches in the middle of the day, unless it was Sunday. Then we had a proper "Sunday dinner"; and sandwiches, and maybe jelly or cake in the evening), each tent group would be given the whole afternoon to go off site and practise whatever we were doing for the Campfire show on Sunday evening. This could include a short play, or a ditty or two; even a solo performance on behalf of your group if you had the confidence.

The second and final Saturday had arrived all too soon for all of us. I certainly wasn't looking forward to leaving, as I had been earlier in the week. I loved this holiday now, and so did everyone else. It was a brilliant place to be; lots of fun and games, with plenty of exercise and good grub too. Who could want more? Even the nights were okay.

Time flies, especially when you don't want it to. We'd had our lunch and done the washing up (even that wasn't the chore it seemed when I first arrived here), and now it was time for tent inspection, the second of the day! Skipper reminded us that Camp was almost over (no need for that, mister) so precious "tent marks" would be hard to gain, but easy to lose. Almost everyone was into the tent competition, so did anything and everything to stay in the running for the coveted title of "Tent Champions 1965". Our tents were always well presented for the twice daily (sometimes more, as in today) inspections, with new and innovative ideas for setting out its contents which would be thoroughly inspected by the Skipper. And when he had posted the scores on the notice board in the marquee, we were off out again to work on our stuff for the Campfire. We all had to find somewhere other groups couldn't see or hear us as we ran through our presentations. Skipper said there would be lots of guests turning up for the Campfire, and it was important to impress them all, because some of the invited guests would be judging our performances. Eh? Oh yes......tent marks. Let's get to it then, lads!

Later, we were treated to a lovely beef stew which most of us really enjoyed. For me, the food was delicious. Our mom was a very good cook, but she couldn't afford to feed us a hot meal every day. And when we did have hot food it was either rabbit; or breast of lamb stew mainly. It was good wholesome food, and cheap then. Here we were served like kings, with second helpings the norm.

So we'd had dinner, and the washing up was completed. We were looking forward to a few games on the field (in the marquee if the weather was poor) after another tent inspection (blimey Skip') and maybe a walk in the valley... maybe??

It was growing darker. The sun had danced its merry course over the Long Mynd and sunk below the near horizon. Darkness; real and proper darkness comes swiftly and unmercifully in the deep countryside. Skipper called us all into the marquee, which was lit only by a couple of lanterns. He explained slowly that it was approaching the time when we would all go down into the valley of Minton Batch to see if we could spot the ghosts!! Bleedin' 'ell. Going home didn't seem such a bad idea now!

We were advised to go and get some warm clothes on, even trousers if we wanted. It had been shorts-only so far, so it must be twice as cold in that valley at night! My thoughts were confirmed when we got back to Skipper because he said that IF the ghosts were about, it would be freezing in the valley. He began to tell us the story of why and how the ghosts... a man and a woman... came to haunt the valley on the second Saturday of August every year. Skip told us about two lovers meeting on the second bridge and re-enacting some sort of tragic happening hundreds of years ago. I didn't hear all of the story because by now wild imagination had completely gripped my mind! Apparently, if these ghosts could be "encircled by a chain of human sympathy, in complete silence" (Skip's words) "their tormented souls would find everlasting peace together".

Okay, yes; right, then. This'll be easy won't it, eh? NO!

We DIDN'T manage it... and who could wonder why? We shit ourselves to a man! The ghosts did appear, and it was very, very scary. I was actually holding onto Skipper's hand like many others, and we could feel it shaking like a leaf. A bloody great big copper scared stiff, so what chance did we have if they attacked us! Last one back to Camp is a cissy. No-one came last!

In all the tents that night, stories were told of how the ghosts had touched us as we made our way back to Camp in the dark. How we'd seen one on a horse; the one Skipper told us about in the story. He had ridden the horse straight through us. Honest...

Sunday morning dawned, bringing our last full day at this beautiful place. And it was the busiest day of the whole ten-day holiday. Church first; followed by another chance to practise for the evening's entertainment around the campfire. A big square was dug out of the field between the marquee and the tents. This was Mr Rudge's job, as was the fetching of logs to burn later. Mr Rudge was leader of Tent Three, but he also helped the Skipper a lot; sorting this and that to keep the Camp rolling along.

After Sunday dinner it was time for the "Scavenge Hunt". We were sent off Camp with another tent leader to find all sorts of weird objects. We also had to find out some facts about the surrounding area (certain phone numbers, etc.), and Skipper's date of birth, amongst other things. If we didn't find this out properly, we were asked, by Skipper to guess the year he was born. That always created fun and laughter. 'Er, 1896'; Erm 1777'; 'What bout 1969?' Those guesses really tickled our Skipper; he laughed out loud, and it made us boys laugh as well.

At the end of the jaunt over the hills and through the lanes, we had to give a good reason for Skip to let us back in Camp. Was he daft... we lived there! I often wonder how we all eventually got back into Camp because he was very strict with that little gem.

With Skipper insisting on us all having silly reasons to re-enter Camp, it threw us back regarding the programme. So the fancy dress competition was rushed; a shambles, I think.

And then... after a quick bite, and the dreaded, but final tent inspection, the moment arrived: Campfire!!!

Loads of folk known to Skipper and other members of staff rolled into our little piece of England to join in celebrating our ten days at Camp. They watched us perform (badly) our plays and skits, etc.; some even clapped us. It was a truly fantastic and memorable finale to a brilliant holiday. Skipper and his merry band of volunteers had looked after us, and cared for us as if we were their real children all the way through this great ride; thank you all, especially the big copper! There were one or two coppers on site, actually.

The final morning dawned, a sad day; home time. And whilst I was looking forward to getting back to my mom, she wouldn't have minded waiting another ten days. But a ticking clock waits for nothing and no-one, and that's a shame. After a small breakfast (because of the long coach journey ahead) and the travel sickness pills had been swallowed by those who thought they needed them, we hung around the campsite in the clothes we had arrived in, just killing time until the coach arrived. New friendships were made; some of them about to end, at least for twelve months; tears, and promises to 'keep in touch'. It all *happened during those final moments of my first time at the WVS Boys Camp.*

When we were all boarded, and sat down, Skipper got on the coach, and so did some of the staff, to say a personal cheerio to each of us. The tears flowed just like the brook to our left and right. We would be taking our tears with us but the brook, the lucky brook, was staying in this beautiful place forever!

God bless all the staff and helpers who worked so well together, to give us all the time of our young lives. Especially, the big copper!!

Alan Scriven; aged 12.
The Bell Tent (Four)

Epilogue

I sincerely hope that the reader has enjoyed this second and final book on The Longmynd Adventure Camp, and events in my life since its inception, to the present day. It has been for me a truly wonderful experience. To be honest I didn't dare dream that I would see my words in published form. I decided to write about the Camp's first forty years because it was (sadly now when I look back) then, 1998, that I ended my association with the charity, just for something to do really but something that would examine my skill and ability to write. Fortunately, I kept every single document that came into my possession whilst I was a part of the Camp and doing this, combined with the help of Bill Williams and Pete Roberts, who both very kindly gave me what documents they had, assisted me no end in writing a true and concise history.

The Longmynd Adventure Camp changed a lot of people's lives. Not just the lads who were lucky enough to be selected; some, like me, time and time again. As well, many of the kind souls who came along at different parts of the Camps then life, willingly offering whatever they could to help the lads enjoy the experience; the truly unforgettable experience that this now sixty-year-old organisation gave to everyone who was ever a part of it.

The format was simple: to give kids less fortunate than others (in that they wouldn't be able to have any other holiday) a basic camping holiday in the beautiful countryside of South Shropshire.

On behalf of all the children who came, and thoroughly enjoyed their ten days of unique adventure, over the forty years before everything changed, I would like to offer my sincere thanks to every one of the folk (whether living or resting in peace), too numerous to mention individually, who made it continually possible.

The Camp was a major part of my life between 1965 and 1998. It's no lie to say now that it has been, really, since. Although I am no longer an actual part of it, it will always be in my blood; and in the blood of many others like me who still take pleasure in reminiscing: what we did; where we went; the people we met, etc. That will never end, because there are always new stories, and more camping in the batch.

Whenever I hear the name 'Minton Batch' a little phrase pops into my head. Many years ago, Skipper Bill Williams' eldest daughter Ann went away on a short break whilst the Camp was in full swing. And one day, our Skipper called me into his caravan and said he had received a letter from Ann.

Ann had visited her dad on Camp lots of times from a very early age, as had Debbie, her younger sister. Well, Ann would have obviously preferred to be at Camp rather than wherever she was because in her letter to her dad she said so: "It's okay here Dad I suppose, but I'd rather be in Minton Batch; oh for Minton Batch!" This phrase always springs to mind when I hear the name of that beautiful place.

Finally, and I've said this before, but I can't help repeating how I, and most others who were a major part of the Longmynd Adventure Camp, have been utterly ignored whenever the Camp's illustrious past is mentioned by any of the current committee, or in its so-called *Dawn Chorus* offerings. At Bill Williams' memorial service Don Rogers and I had a good, lengthy chat about general stuff. And towards the end of our conversation I told him how I felt about the fact that my time and efforts for the greater good of the Camp had been totally erased from its history. I even said that this was another reason why I was writing the true history myself. Don very graciously denied my claims; but could give me no answers when I challenged him to give me an example. I trust and hope the reader doesn't consider that maybe I am looking to have "my trumpet blown for me"; I'm not. And anyway, hardly any of the current committee will know who I am (unless they have read my first book). Don said he was going to treat himself to a copy, and I hope he did. But I can't say for certain whether he did or not because there's been no contact between us since.

I know, appreciate and accept that I was just one cog in a big wheel. And I am in no way suggesting that I did more than most others just because of my progress from child beneficiary to 'Skipper'. But surely that achievement ought to have at least a small part in the history of The Longmynd Adventure Camp. It was, and will always be, the best 'journey' of my whole life.

Thanks again to everyone who in whatever way contributed to this book; and my first book, *The Longmynd Adventure Camp and Me*.

God bless you all.

Finally, if you haven't yet had the pleasure of walking on the Long Mynd; or its valleys and batches, I urge you to do so. You will not be disappointed.

Acknowledgements

Katharine Smith (Heddon Publishing)

Shropshire Newspapers Ltd

Express and Star Newspaper (Wolverhampton and West Midlands)

PC Bill Newbound. Camp Staff 1959; 1960

Mrs Miriam Newbound. Camp Staff (kitchen) 1959

Miss Heather Perkins. Camp Staff (kitchen) 1959

Mr Tony Price. Camp Staff

Mr Pete Roberts. Camp Staff (Contributor to this book)

Mr Malcolm Webster. Camp Staff (Contributor to this book)

Mr Richard Edwards. Camp Staff

Mr Les Beddoes (Bishops Castle). Loan of Marquee 1960s and 70s.

Mr M Bowen. Camp Staff

Mr E Williams. Camp Staff

Mr K Wall (Licensee: The Old Gate Inn, Claverley) Promotion of book sales

Mr J Cully. Camp Staff

Mr B Jones. Camp Staff

Mr R Howell. (Director, Intermediate Treatment Fund) Appeal 1978.

Mr Ross (of Smetcott). Loan of cottage for Camp 1963; Picklescott).

Bishop Mark (Hereford Cathedral). Official Opening of Kitchen/Staffroom building in 1966.

Brow Farm, nr Stiperstones (overnight camping 1990)

Ms Christine Harte (former wife of the author). Supporting my work with the Camp.

The Llankelly Trust

The Walker Trust of Shropshire

Mr R Howell (Director, Intermediate Treatment Fund)

If you would like to contact the author you can email him here: alan.scriv53@gmail.com

If you have enjoyed this book, please consider leaving a review for this book on Amazon, Goodreads, or any other review site or group you are linked with. It's invaluable for a book's reputation, it may help another reader decide whether they would like to read the book, and above all it will put a smile on the face of a hardworking author!

www.ingramcontent.com/pod-product-compliance
Lightning Source LLC
Chambersburg PA
CBHW031120020426
42333CB00012B/158